RIVERS of the WORLD

The Nile

Titles in the Rivers of the World series include:

RIVERS
of the
WORLD

The Nile

James Barter

LUCENT
BOOKS®

THOMSON
━━━━✳━━━━
GALE

San Diego • Detroit • New York • San Francisco • Cleveland • New Haven, Conn. • Waterville, Maine • London • Munich

THOMSON

✦ ™

GALE

LIBRARY OF CONGRESS CATALOGING-IN-PUBLICATION DATA

Barter, James, 1946–
    The Nile / by James Barter.
        p. cm. — (Rivers of the world)
Includes bibliographical references and index.
Summary: Describes the Nile River from ancient times to the present, and discusses what must be done to protect and preserve this river.
    ISBN 1-56006-935-X (hardback : alk. paper)
    1. Nile River Valley—Juvenile literature. 2. Nile River—Juvenile literature. [1. Nile River Valley. 2. Nile River.] I. Title. II. Rivers of the world (Lucent Books)
    DT116 .B27 2003
    962—dc21

2001007679

Contents

· · · · · · · · · · · · ·

Foreword

· · · · · · · · · · · ·

Human history and rivers are inextricably intertwined. Of all the geologic wonders of nature, none has played a more central and continuous role in the history of civilization than rivers. Fanning out across every major landmass except the Antarctic, all great rivers wove an arterial network that played a pivotal role in the inception of early civilizations and in the evolution of today's modern nation-states.

More than ten thousand years ago, when nomadic tribes first began to settle into small, stable communities, they discovered the benefits of cultivating crops and domesticating animals. These incipient civilizations developed a dependence on continuous flows of water to nourish and sustain their communities and food supplies. As small agrarian towns began to dot the Asian and African continents, the importance of rivers escalated as sources of community drinking water, as places for washing clothes, for sewage removal, for food, and as means of transportation. One by one, great riparian civilizations evolved whose collective fame is revered today, including ancient Mesopotamia, between the Tigris and Euphrates Rivers; Egypt, along the Nile; India, along the Ganges and Indus Rivers; and China, along the Yangtze. Later, for the same reasons, early civilizations in the Americas gravitated to the major rivers of the New World such as the Amazon, Mississippi, and Colorado.

For thousands of years, these rivers admirably fulfilled their role in nature's cycle of birth, death, and renewal. The waters also supported the rise of nations and their expanding populations. As hundreds and then thousands of cities sprang up along major rivers, today's modern nations emerged and discovered modern uses for the rivers. With more mouths to feed than ever before, great irrigation canals supplied by river water fanned out across the landscape, transforming parched land into mile upon mile of fertile cropland. Engineers developed the mathematics needed to throw great concrete dams across rivers to control occasional flooding and to store trillions of gallons of water to irrigate crops during the hot summer months. When the great age of electricity arrived, engineers added to the demands placed on rivers by using their cascading water to drive huge hydroelectric turbines to light and heat homes and skyscrapers in urban settings. Rivers also played a major role in the development of modern factories as sources of water for processing a variety of commercial goods and as a convenient place to discharge various types of refuse.

For a time, civilizations and rivers functioned in harmony. Such a benign relationship, however, was not destined to last. At the end of the twentieth century, scientists confirmed the opinions of environmentalists: The viability of all major rivers of the world was threatened. Urban populations could no longer drink the fetid water, masses of fish were dying from chemical toxins, and microorganisms critical to the food chain were disappearing along with the fish species at the top of the chain. The great hydroelectric dams had altered the natural flow of rivers, blocking migratory fish routes. As the twenty-first century unfolds, all who have contributed to spoiling the rivers are now in agreement that immediate steps must be taken to heal the rivers if their partnership with civilization is to continue.

Each volume in the Lucent Rivers of the World series tells the unique and fascinating story of a great river and its people. The significance of rivers to civilizations is emphasized to highlight both their historical role and the present situation. Each volume illustrates the idiosyncrasies of one great river in terms of its physical attributes, the plants and animals that depend on it, its role in ancient and modern cultures, how it served the needs of the people, the misuse of the river, and steps now being taken to remedy its problems.

Introduction

• • • • • • • • • • • • • • • • •

The Centrality of the Nile

For more than five thousand years the Egyptians have owed their existence to a river that begins its journey more than four thousand miles to the south, deep in the rain-drenched highlands of equatorial Africa. During the summer, ancient Egyptians awaited the annual flooding of the Nile that washed across their fields, depositing nutrients that made the Nile Delta the most productive farmland in the ancient world. It is the abundance of Egypt's annual Nile-enriched crop that was referred to by one of the Old Testament writers who noted thousands of years ago that there was famine elsewhere but in Egypt there was bread.

Nothing was more central in the lives and culture of the ancient Egyptians than the Nile. Although they did not understand where the river came from or how it brought them their well-being, they nonetheless understood that it consistently did so. Out of respect and appreciation for this gift, they included the Nile in their pantheon of gods. Egyptians prayed to the river, sacrificed to it, painted pictures of it on temple walls, and wrote poetry in praise of its magical waters.

The Nile is undeniably even more central in the lives of modern dwellers along its banks than it was in ancient times. Today, several giant dams span the Nile providing hydroelectricity, canals crisscross areas of the desert providing water for new crops, and modern irrigation pumps provide billions of gallons of water so that farmers can grow grain, vegetables, and fresh fruit year-round. Industries have set up operations along the banks of the Nile to use its waters for cleaning and processing many products, tour boats and floating hotels travel its waters, and Nile water flows through the plumbing of modern skyscrapers and apartment houses in many urban centers. As it did in the past, the Nile serves as a sewer, although today it annually receives thousands of tons of chemical wastes that are killing its fish, plants, and the very crops it waters.

Three men paddle up the Nile in Sudan, one of the ten nations that depend on the river to provide water for drinking, agriculture, and industry.

As the twenty-first century begins, more is being asked of the Nile than ever before. Ten nations now share its gift, and although the volume of the Nile remains massive, it can no longer satisfy the needs of the 300 million people whose demands for water continually increase.

The job of healing the Nile falls to the ten nations that share and depend on its gift in a complex relationship of water sharing and river diversions that include dams and canals. From the Nile's origins in equatorial Africa to its mouth along the Mediterranean, all of the Nile nations are now contributing to an improved understanding of the limits of the river and the future use of its life-giving water. At this time, everyone agrees that regaining and sustaining the ecological balance of the Nile is critical to maintaining the river's ability to nurture the lives of those who depend on its water. Steps are being taken to help the Nile, but whether enough can be done soon enough is a matter of disagreement among experts. What is not subject to debate is the Nile's leading role in the lives of peoples past and present.

1

· · · · · · · · · ·

A River in the Sand

The Nile is the world's longest river, stretching and meandering from equatorial Africa up the eastern side of the African continent to empty into the Mediterranean Sea, a journey of 4,160 miles. Extremely rare among the great rivers of the world, the Nile flows in a northerly direction.

The Nile is also unusual in that it is the only significant river to flow through a major desert. The early Egyptians referred to the Nile as "the River in the Sand" because, to them, the river appeared to well up from the sands of the Sahara Desert. What the ancient Egyptians did not know was that the Nile gathers nearly all of its water during the first half of its journey as it courses through the wet tropical uplands of equatorial Africa. During the second half of its journey, as it crosses the burning sands of the northern African deserts, the Nile loses billions of gallons of water to evaporation. Of the major rivers of the world, the Nile is the only one that loses more than half of its volume to evaporation before reaching its ocean destination.

Still, the amount of water the Nile delivers at its mouth staggers the imagination. In spite of the loss to evaporation,

Palm trees are partially submerged during the annual flooding of the Nile in 1962. Dams along the Nile now control the floods.

hydrology professor Daniel Hillel estimates, "The maximum flood stage normally arrives in mid-September, when the flow rate may exceed 700 million cubic meters [915 million cubic yards] a day."[1] Converted to gallons, this one-day volume is a phenomenal 62 billion.

This annual late summer flood, a characteristic that is unique to the Nile, is one of the sources of the river's fame. Although the annual flood is now controlled by a system of dams, for five thousand years this inundation was welcomed by farmers along the Lower Nile since it was the only water most of their crops would receive all year.

To the ancient Egyptians, both the flooding of the Nile and the source of its waters were mysteries. Yet even though they benefited from the river, the people of ancient Egypt made little effort to determine its source. Modern historians believe that although the annual flood varied in intensity, because it arrived every year, where it came from was of little concern for ancient Egyptians.

A River of Rivers

Even had the ancient Egyptians tried to trace the Nile to its source, they would have faced a challenging task.

Papyrus

In ancient Egypt papyrus, *Cyperus papyrus,* had a variety of uses, making it the most versatile plant in Egypt and second to wheat as the most important crop. Growing wild and in profusion within the Nile Delta, papyrus is a reed-type plant that grows on long stalks to a height of twenty feet. The long, fibrous stalks were cut into long strips and were woven to make utilitarian commodities such as boats, ropes, baskets, boxes, mats, sandals, and even furniture. However, of all of the useful consumer goods, it is most well known for the contribution it made to learning and education as the earliest form of writing paper.

For thousands of years papyrus was the most economical and commonly used product for writing books, recording laws, and signing contracts. No substitution for papyrus paper could be found that was as durable and lightweight until the development of pulped paper by the Arabs during the twelfth century A.D.

Papyrus was manufactured using the following process:

• The stalks of the papyrus plant are harvested.
• The green skin of the stalk is peeled off and the inner pith is taken out and cut into long strips. The strips are then pounded and soaked in water for three days until pliable.
• The strips are then cut to the length desired and are laid horizontally on a cotton sheet slightly overlapping. Other strips are laid vertically over the horizontal strips, resulting in the crosshatch pattern in papyrus paper. Another cotton sheet is then placed on top.
• The sheet is put in a press and is squeezed together, with the cotton sheets being replaced until all of the moisture is removed.
• Finally, all of the strips are pressed together, forming a single sheet of papyrus paper.

Modern geographers and hydrologists point out that this colossal waterway is not one continuous river from beginning to end. Rather, its flow consists of a complex tapestry of hundreds of tributaries that weave and twist their way together to form larger rivers, which in turn combine with other rivers to eventually create the Nile. In this

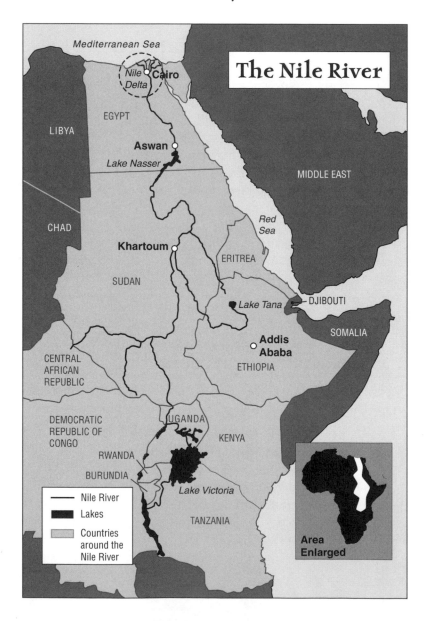

The Nile River

Mediterranean Sea

Nile Delta — Cairo

EGYPT

LIBYA

Aswan

Lake Nasser

MIDDLE EAST

CHAD

Red Sea

Khartoum

ERITREA

SUDAN

Lake Tana — DJIBOUTI

SOMALIA

Addis Ababa

CENTRAL AFRICAN REPUBLIC

ETHIOPIA

DEMOCRATIC REPUBLIC OF CONGO

UGANDA

KENYA

RWANDA

BURUNDIA

Lake Victoria

TANZANIA

— Nile River
■ Lakes
□ Countries around the Nile River

Area Enlarged

regard, the Nile is more accurately described as a system of rivers—a river of rivers.

Why the Nile takes the path it does has until relatively recently been another mystery. Although the Red Sea and Indian Ocean are closer to the many tributaries of the Nile than the Mediterranean is, the river moves north rather than east. Geologists explain this unusual phenomenon as the result of tectonic forces that thrust the African continent up in the south, creating a gradual downhill slope from equatorial Africa to the Mediterranean.

Modern-day maps and satellite photographs of the Nile basin reveal a network of rivers and streams working their way to the sea. They also reveal that the Nile's three largest tributaries south of Egypt are the White Nile, the Blue Nile, and the Atbara which combine to form the main body of the Nile as it flows through upper Sudan and Egypt.

The White Nile

The White Nile, known in Arabic Al-Bahr al-Abyad, is considered the main branch of the Nile because its source, Lake Victoria, lies farther from the river's mouth than the sources of the other two largest tributaries. Lake Victoria has been accepted as the Nile's source by the public ever since its naming by British explorer John Speke in 1858. More recently, however, a small river named the Kagera was discovered that flows into Lake Victoria, so there remains some controversy as to what constitutes the ultimate source of the Nile.

In any case, Lake Victoria's imposing size at 27,000 square miles makes it the second-largest freshwater lake in the world, and its massive outpour of water, which feeds the Nile at an average daily rate of roughly 66 million cubic yards of water, makes Lake Victoria the Nile's single largest source. This volume is even more remarkable considering that hydrologists estimate that Lake Victoria loses approximately 72 percent of its water through evaporation.

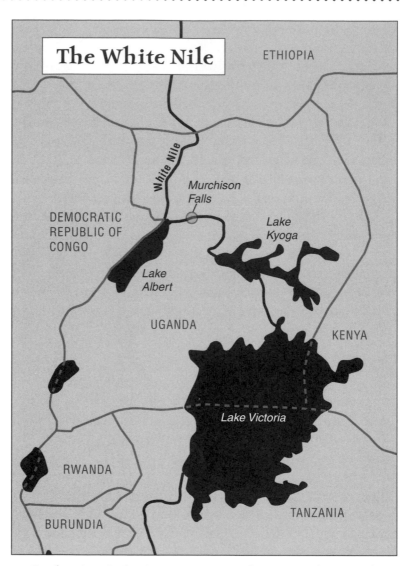

The White Nile

ETHIOPIA

White Nile

Murchison
Falls

Lake
Kyoga

DEMOCRATIC
REPUBLIC OF
CONGO

Lake
Albert

UGANDA

KENYA

Lake Victoria

RWANDA

BURUNDIA

TANZANIA

On leaving Lake Victoria at an elevation of 3,700 feet, the Nile drops precipitously at a ratio of 1:1,302; that is, for every 1,302 feet of horizontal run, the river's elevation drops one foot. This severe slope sends the Nile cascading for 300 miles over rapids and cataracts, making this stretch of the river unnavigable. The river at this point flows first north, and then abruptly turns west, until it enters Lake Albert, which borders both Uganda and the Democratic Republic of the Congo. This lake is slightly more than 2,000 square miles and sits at an elevation of about 2,000 feet. Unlike Lake Victoria, Albert is narrow and deep, which, combined with its lower elevation, means that most of the water that enters the lake exits as the Nile continues northward, rather than being lost to evaporation. As a result, the average daily outflow is about 59 million cubic yards. The river drains from the northern end of Lake Albert and flows through northern Uganda and enters southern Sudan.

As the White Nile enters southern Sudan, the river begins another rapid descent, cascading through steeply sloping banks and through narrow gorges. In this stretch, as the river moves north, it picks up additional water from hundreds of small tributaries. Hydrologists estimate that the river at this point in its journey, 120 miles north of Lake Albert, adds 17 percent to the volume it had when exiting the lake.

A very peculiar hydrographic phenomenon occurs next. The White Nile suddenly enters a flat, wide, clay-lined basin 40,000 square miles in area called the Sudd, an Arabic word meaning "the Barrier." Here, the slope of the Nile drops to a ratio of about 1:14,000, and the flow slows dramatically, creating the largest swamp in the world. Soaked year-round, the Sudd is a patchwork of marshes, bogs, and ponds densely packed with every imaginable aquatic plant.

The Sudd is aptly named: The combination of water, plants, and heat attracts one of the world's largest collections of insects carrying so many different diseases that human habitation there is a near impossibility. Indeed, few people ever attempt to travel in the Sudd since the mass of plant life makes the waterway nearly impassable.

The Sudd lies just north of the equator and bakes in the African heat all year long, causing a massive loss of water to evaporation. As the river pushes its way through the Sudd, half of its water evaporates, which annually adds up to about 28 billion cubic yards, but it can reach 34 billion cubic yards.

In spite of the evaporation, the Sudd never dries up because numerous tributary rivers flow into it. The net effect of evaporation and additional inflow is the emergence of the rivers from the Sudd at the daily rate of about 69 million cubic yards. By the time the water moves out of the Sudd, it has acquired a milky-white color from which the White Nile takes its name. The discoloration is caused by the presence of millions of tons of decayed organic matter picked up in the swamp. For the next five hundred miles, the White Nile flows north, until it arrives at Khartoum, the modern-day capital of Sudan, where it joins the Blue Nile.

The Blue Nile

The Blue Nile, in Arabic Al-Bahr al-Azraq, meaning "Blue Water," was so named because of its high content of mineral sediment, which makes it markedly darker than the White Nile. This tributary of the Nile captures all of the runoff water from the Ethiopian highlands and descends into Lake Tana, about twelve hundred square miles, at an elevation of over seven thousand feet. As the Blue Nile departs Lake Tana, it begins its descent flowing south, then it turns abruptly due west, and finally north. Eventually the Blue Nile meets the White Nile at Khartoum.

During the flood season during midsummer, the Blue Nile accounts for as much as 90 percent of the combined Nile's flow. Indeed, the volume of the Blue Nile during the annual flood is so great that when it joins the White Nile in Khartoum, it actually pushes back its waters, creating a temporary lake forty to fifty miles long. For the remainder of the year, however, the flow of the Blue Nile decreases to little more than 1.3 million cubic yards a day.

The Atbara

Two hundred miles north of Khartoum, the last major tributary of the Nile, the Atbara River, joins the other tributaries at the city of Atbara. This river drains the

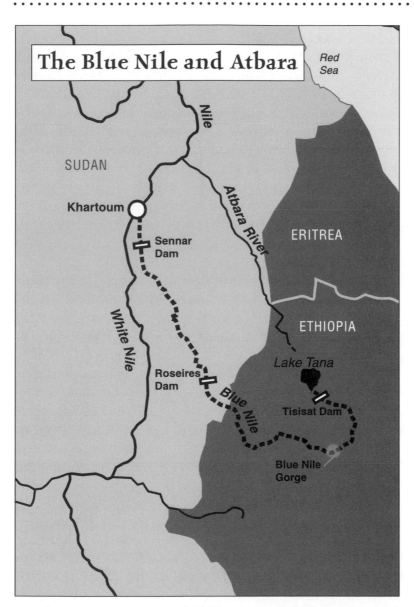

The Blue Nile and Atbara

northwest mountains of Ethiopia and Eritrea, located north of Lake Tana. Of the three principal tributaries, this one is the smallest, contributing about 66 million cubic yards per day during the flood season. Befitting its smaller size and unlike the other two major Nile tributaries, which flow year-round, during the hot arid season the Atbara becomes a long mud puddle.

The Main Nile

From Atbara to the Mediterranean, a distance of about 1,500 miles, the Nile threads its way through the Sahara Desert. In spite of considerable evaporation without gaining additional volume from any significant tributaries, this is the stretch where the Nile makes its best-known and most significant contribution to the peoples of the Nile basin. It is along most of this last stretch that the Nile's slope drops to 1:13,000, allowing the water to spread out from 0.25 of a mile to 2 miles on either side to nourish cropland, creating a narrow band of greenery in an otherwise inhospitable land.

Despite the evaporation that takes place as the river courses through the desert, the Nile remains a formidable waterway. Annually, the total flow at Aswan, in southern Egypt, is estimated to be more than 100 billion cubic yards.

As soon as the Nile reaches Cairo, the modern-day capital of Egypt, the geography of the river changes dramatically one last time. The two-mile band of greenbelt disappears, and the Nile's slope drops to its lowest ratio, 1:20,000. Here, the waters of the Nile fan out, creating a triangular flood plane called the Nile Delta, before spilling into the Mediterranean.

The Nile Delta

The Nile Delta is the last leg of the four-thousand-mile journey to the sea. The delta, a broad, flat plane where the rich soil produces high-yield crops, is the result of the annual flooding of the Nile. The early first-century A.D. Greek historian and geographer Strabo described the verdant Nile Delta as having seven river arteries, like fingers, fanning out from Cairo to the Mediterranean and creating the delta. As the water funnels down the seven arteries, the water is efficiently distributed across the delta, where farmers grow crops such as wheat, corn, figs, and olives.

The Geology of the Nile

Geologists say that during the geologic period called the Tertiary, about 30 million years ago, the Nile was a much shorter river, perhaps originating in northwestern Ethiopia or just north of where the Sudd begins today. The length of the Nile at that time would have been about two thousand miles.

Geologic evidence suggests that roughly 5 million years later the system of lakes that today includes Lakes Victoria and Albert developed a northern outlet caused by excessive flooding. This northern outlet released a flood, creating the enormous Lake Sudd, which today is a swamp. Over 3 to 5 million years, Lake Sudd began to silt up, causing its water level to rise and spill over into many tributaries that later formed the White Nile.

As the White Nile increased in size and volume, its northern flow eventually merged with the flow of the Blue Nile at Khartoum. The confluence of these two major rivers created the Nile that rushed downstream toward the Mediterranean Sea. Coincidental with the formation of the Nile, the narrow channel connecting the Mediterranean Sea with the Atlantic at present-day Gibraltar closed. Without a steady inflow of water from the Atlantic, the warm waters of the Mediterranean quickly evaporated, causing the flow of the Nile to accelerate downhill and cutting deep canyons along its course through Egypt.

Roughly 13 million years ago, the strip of land at Gibraltar reopened, sending a massive inundation of water rushing into the Mediterranean that flooded all of its coastlines and dramatically forced saltwater to wash up the Nile as far as Aswan. Over the next several million years, as the level of the Mediterranean declined, the canyons, which had already been carved by the river, began to fill with silt, and the river leveled out to the gentle slope it has today.

The Nile that peoples of the African continent see today is very similar to what early inhabitants saw ten thousand years ago. Although there have been climatic changes such as occasional long periods of droughts and contrasting periods of exceptionally heavy equatorial rains, the geology of the river has remained relatively stable.

A satellite image shows the Nile Delta, where the Nile funnels down seven river arteries and out to the sea.

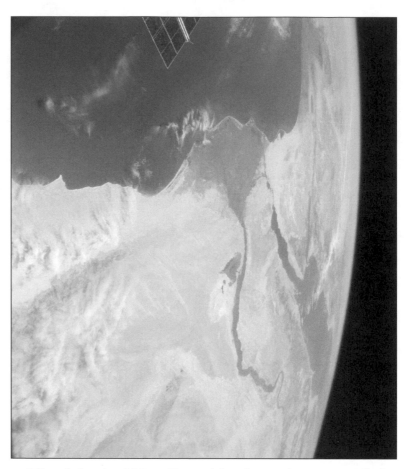

The delta is 120 miles wide along the coast of the Mediterranean, narrowing to an inland point at modern-day Cairo, 100 miles from the coast. This 6,000 square mile parcel of land is the largest and most productive farmland anywhere on the Nile. The delta's importance to Egypt is hard to overstate. The delta and the narrow strip of farmland along the Nile south of Cairo constitute just 3 percent of Egypt's land but account for 99 percent of its farmland. For thousands of years, this land faithfully produced bountiful crops following the annual floods.

The Annual Flood

Of the many attributes of the Nile, the annual flood is its best known. Although all rivers may flood from time to time, the midsummer flooding of the Nile is highly predictable. Moreover, unlike the flooding of other rivers, the Nile's flood was welcomed by those who lived along its banks.

For the thousands of years before engineers began building dams on the Nile, the annual flood was the most

Herodotus Explains the Annual Flood

When Herodotus made his historic visit to Egypt around 476 B.C., he wandered throughout the northern part of the country speaking with all of the educated men he could find about Egyptian history and the country's geography. Of particular interest to Herodotus was the Nile and, specifically, its annual flood. In book two of his history, The Persian Wars, *he recorded some of the Egyptian explanations for the flood—winds and melting snow—and dismissed all of them as fanciful. He then proceeded to give his own equally fanciful explanation that the sun is the cause.*

I will therefore proceed to explain what I think to be the reason of the Nile's swelling in the summer time. During the winter, the sun is driven out of his usual course by the storms, and removes to the upper parts of Libya. This is the whole secret in the fewest possible words; for it stands to reason that the country to which the Sun-god approaches the nearest, and which he passes most directly over, will be scantiest of water, and that there the streams which feed the rivers will shrink the most. . . .

And my own opinion is that the sun does not get rid of all the water which he draws year by year from the Nile, but retains some about him. When the winter begins to soften, the sun goes back again to his old place in the middle of the heaven, and proceeds to attract water equally from all countries. Till then the other rivers run big, from the quantity of rain-water which they bring down from countries where so much moisture falls that all the land is cut into gullies; but in summer, when the showers fail, and the sun attracts their water, they become low. The Nile, on the contrary, not deriving any of its bulk from rains, and being in winter subject to the attraction of the sun, naturally runs at that season, unlike all other streams, with a less burden of water than in the summer time.

celebrated event of the year. Beginning in late July and lasting until September, the Nile would swell and overflow its banks, saturating the adjoining lands. During the flood, everyone living near the river headed for higher ground as the water spread across the land. In the Nile Delta, the river spread across both banks for fifty miles in either direction.

In ancient times, seasonal festivals marked the arrival of the flood and sacrifices were made to the river deities. Ironically, the ancient Egyptians never understood the cause of the flood to which they owed their existence. The great flood was not understood until the source of the Nile was discovered. It is now known that the annual flood is the result of heavy spring rainfall far to the south, which swells the Nile tributaries, increasing its volume as the rushing waters enter Lower Egypt. As the downward slope suddenly levels out near the Mediterranean, the gushing water spills over its bank in the delta and inundates the land for miles. Roughly two months later, after the water has saturated the land and the floodwaters recede, the land is ready to be planted.

The importance of the Nile extends beyond its allowing people to grow food. As is the case with all rivers, the Nile is home to a remarkably abundant collection of animals and plants that play an important role as a food source to the peoples of the Nile. Many of these species are indigenous to this part of the world and are important for sustaining the ecology of the river.

The Fauna of the Nile

The vast majority of animals dependent on the waters of the Nile inhabit the first two thousand miles in the wet tropical zones of equatorial Africa. To the north, where the river flows through the Sahara, virtually the only animals that can survive are the fish that live in the Nile itself. To the south, besides fish the most common river-dwelling creatures are the hippopotamus, *Hippopotamus amphibius,* and the Nile crocodile, *Crocodilus niloticus.*

Weighing up to four tons, the hippopotamus is the second-largest land animal on Earth, after the elephant. To maintain their bulk, these herbivores graze endlessly on the thick aquatic vegetation that thrives in the Upper Nile. This massive mammal is capable of leaving the river for short periods, but it prefers to graze slowly through the plentiful water hyacinth and river grasses. The hippo is well adapted to its life in the Nile and is capable of remaining submerged on the river bottom for up to twenty-five minutes while eating. Still, hippos are surprisingly quick on their stubby legs and so have few natural enemies. The local natives occasionally hunt hippos, but they risk much when they do. In fact, humans suffer more deaths from hippos' powerful jaws and trampling feet than from any other animal along the Upper Nile.

Just as fearsome is the Nile crocodile. This large carnivore feeds on animals that carelessly venture too far into the water to drink. Completely submerged except for its eyeballs and tiny nostrils, this reptile, which can weigh as much as a ton, silently creeps close to the riverbank only

Hippopotamuses thrive on the dense aquatic vegetation that grows in the Nile's waters.

to erupt in a fury from the water to seize its victim and drag it under water in an instant of violence. Incapable of chewing its meal, the crocodile then violently spins its dead prey in the water to dismember it, then swallows whole sections of its victim's carcass. Crocodiles are capable of fasting for up to a year, but when they feed on animals the size of zebras and wildebeests, mature males are able to eat several hundred pounds in minutes.

The Nile is also home to a large variety of fish, primarily in the upper reaches of the river. None of the species grows to more than four or five feet in length. Still, they play an important role as part of the food chain of the Nile and are an important part of the diet for people living along the river.

As is the case with fish, the Upper Nile is home to many species of birds. Most are attracted to the water because there they can gorge themselves on small fish and use the thick vegetation along the banks as safe nesting environments. The most colorful and unusual of the Nile's birds are the flamingos, *Phoenicopterus ruber roseus,* which

The Nile crocodile preys upon unwary animals that wade into the river to drink.

congregate in the mud to mate and eat. During mating season hundreds of thousands gather along short stretches of the Nile. The birds are so numerous that the river takes on a pink hue when viewed from a distance.

The Flora of the Nile

Most of the flora that thrives in the Nile or on its banks do so along the Upper Nile, where rainfall is plentiful. As the river winds its way north out of the tropics and into the arid Sahara Desert, riparian vegetation declines dramatically.

Satellite photographs of Africa tell a colorful story of the Nile's vegetation. From the source of the Nile in the region of Lake Victoria, photographs reveal light and dark green coloration, indicating vast forests, low-lying swamps, and expansive tracts of grasslands. As the river meanders north, the vivid greens gradually give way to rusty browns indicative of scrub vegetation and short trees less densely packed than those upriver. Finally, as the Nile begins its journey through the Sahara Desert, the color of the land fades to a bleached sandy hue, indicating the total absence of vegetation.

The most abundant plant life along the banks of the Upper Nile are grasses interspersed with trees such as eucalyptus, acacia, mvuli (similar to the oak), dry thorn scrub, and oil palm. Thick stands of trees are relatively rare, however. Forests, once extensive, have been cut down for lumber, except in national parks and in nature reserves.

Some of the most valuable plants flourish directly in the river, such as the water hyacinth, *Hyacinthus orientalis*, and the papyrus, *Cyperus papyrus*. The hyacinth is a favorite food for large herbivores as well as spawning grounds for fish. The papyrus is a versatile plant used in antiquity for both ornamental purposes as well as functional ones, such as making paper, boats, sandals, and rope.

Farther north, where the Lower Nile runs through the Sahara Desert, the annual average rainfall is less than five inches and the temperatures are extreme, ranging between freezing and 130 degrees. Virtually no vegetation survives in this tortured landscape, and few land animals can live as a result.

Although none of those who dwelled along the Nile in ancient times had a comprehensive understanding of the river or the wildlife flourishing in it, they nonetheless had an appreciation for its significance in their lives. As a source of water, food, and transportation, everyone living along the banks of the Nile depended on its continuous flow.

2

· · · · · · · · · ·

The Ancient Nile

In ancient times, no matter where one lived along the Nile on its four-thousand-mile pilgrimage to the Mediterranean, the river was vital to one's existence. For the inhabitants of the Upper Nile, living near its source in rain-soaked equatorial Africa, the river fed them from its treasure trove of fish. For those living in the desert regions of the Lower Nile, however, the river was even more of a life-giving force in that it provided water for vital food crops during the river's annual flood.

Because the Nile was the sole source of water, the value of land was determined by its proximity to the river. The most valued property could expect saturation from the annual flood. The next most valued was the marginal farmland that could expect some water, followed by the land located so far from the river that rarely did any of its water reach it.

The Wealth of the Land

For ancient peoples, the Nile was the center of their lives and they worshiped it as a god. That worship was amply rewarded; not only did the river provide people with the ability to grow food, it provided them the ability to grow food in abundance. So rich was the land within a few miles of the river that sizable surpluses of grain, vegetables, and fruit were available for export to neighboring countries. Many inscriptions from the time of the pharaohs attest to the abundance of the harvest. For example, an inscription from the time of Ramses II, who ruled from 1279 to 1212 B.C., reads, "I [the god Ptah who created the Earth] give to you [Ramses II] constant harvests. . . . The sheaves [bundles of wheat] are like sand, the granaries approach heaven, and the grain heaps are like mountains."[2]

The changing of the seasons was nowhere more dramatic than along the Nile, where flooding rather than rainfall provided water for the crops. The seasonal cycle began in midsummer, when the floodwaters covered the

The Adoration of the Nile

Many ancient poems were written to give thanks to the Nile for nourishing the lands and their peoples. It is believed by Egyptologists that the many poems in praise of the river were the result of the annual flooding. The Nile had many cult images and gods, and sacrifice was made to it at many festivals along its banks on the occasion of its flooding. Accompanying the sacrifices were the reading of these poems of praise and thanksgiving. This poem, quoted in The Nile *by Haggai Erlich and Israel Gershoni, is one of many that express the intrinsic link between the river and the people.*

Hail to thee O Nile, that issues
  from the earth
And comes to keep Egypt alive! . . .
He that waters the meadows that
  he created . . .
He that makes to drink the
  desert . . .
He who makes barley and brings
  emmer [wheat] into being . . .
He who brings grass into being
  for cattle . . .
He who makes every beloved tree
  to grow . . .
O, Nile, verdant art thou, who
  makes man and cattle to live.

The horizontal lines scribed on this stone wall were once used as a nilometer to measure the depth of the Nile.

land under several feet of water. The extent of the flood was critical in determining whether a crop was successful or not. Too much water and the crop would be lost because of excessive saturation. Too little and the crops would wilt and die before they could ripen.

For thousands of years the Egyptians tried to predict the extent of the annual flood with devices known today as nilometers. These simple instruments usually were stone pillars that were located well upriver. The pillars were notched at regular intervals. The ancient Egyptians knew that the number of notches that were covered by water would help them predict whether the farmland farther downriver along the Nile and in the delta would produce abundant crops. If too many or too few notches were under water, starvation might visit the peoples of the Nile.

During the flood, all of the minerals and organic nutrients needed to fertilize the crops would be deposited on the land. Ancient Egyptian farmers knew that their black soil was the result of the highly fertile silt carried by the floodwaters. The nutrients were of two types. First, a healthy mix of minerals from the Ethiopian highlands washed down into the Blue Nile that flowed to Khartoum. There, the minerals mixed with the organic matter flowing out of the Sudd in the White Nile. As the two rivers joined to create the main Nile, the waters mixed these components to create the silt needed for another bountiful harvest.

As the swollen river moved north into the Sahara Desert, the floodwaters overflowed the banks, spilling the nutrient-rich water onto Egyptian farmland. Farmers headed for high ground with their animals, where they waited until the water receded. Over thousands of years, an enormous amount of soil was deposited. Modern geologists and agronomists studying the Nile Delta have drilled core samples and report that the silt ranges between thirty and fifty feet in depth.

Farming the Delta

As the floodwaters began to recede, farmers sought to capture as much of the river as possible to irrigate the land so as to ensure a bountiful harvest. The earliest method of irrigation was called basin irrigation, which was accomplished by dividing the fields along the river into a series of basins separated from one another by earthen dikes. If the flood was low one year, the dikes were opened and the basins were allowed to flood

under several feet of water. The openings in the dikes were then closed, trapping the water in the basins and allowing it to soak down many feet into the soil. After several weeks, the river would recede and the excess water would evaporate, leaving the basins ready for planting.

A worker harvesting his crop is portrayed in this ancient Egyptian tomb painting.

Herodotus observed this simple system of irrigation and recognized that it allowed farmers to grow more food with less effort: "At present, it must be confessed, they [Egyptians in the delta] obtain the fruits of the field with less trouble than any other people in the world, the rest of the Egyptians included. . . . Nor do they do any of the work which the rest of mankind find necessary if they are to get a crop."[3]

As the soil began to dry, farmers prepared it for planting by ploughing the fields with oxen or humans, scattering seeds, and waiting for them to ripen three months later. When the harvest time came, farmers swung curved sickles to cut the grain stalks, then they would separate the seeds from the stalks. This process of separation, called threshing, was accomplished by cattle walking on

Rope Stretchers

When the floodwaters receded in late September and early October, the fields in the delta were soaked in rich nutrients, but all indicators of who the land belonged to had been washed away. The farmers' first job upon returning to their land was therefore to reestablish land boundaries. Determining where one farmer's land ended and another's began fell to men called rope stretchers, who functioned as Egyptian surveyors.

To reestablish land boundaries, rope stretchers were employed to redraw property lines erased each year by the annual flood. Early surveying equipment such as the *groma* were apparently useful on flat terrain and a small range of angles. The *groma* consists of stones hanging from the ends of two sticks set at right angles to one another. As the rope stretcher held the *groma* still, the sun would cast a shadow on the ground of the four stones and the two sticks.

This shadow created two four-foot-long lines, and by aligning the hanging stones with some distant object, such as a large rock or tree, the rope stretcher could scratch a line in the dirt establishing boundary lines.

Long before the sixth-century B.C. Greek mathematician Pythagoras, the Egyptians redrew boundary markers using their understanding of geometry. They knew, for example, that the shortest distance between two points on the land was a straight line, and they understood and could determine right angles.

With this simple understanding of geometry, each year rope stretchers redrew land boundaries by establishing a fixed point and then using offsets from these fixed points of known distances and known angles. In this way, rope stretchers could start their boundary measurements at the same point following each annual flood to ensure that farmers worked the same piece of land each year.

the wheat and knocking the grain off the stalks. The farmers then gathered the grain and hauled it to market.

Wheat was the staple crop along the Nile but by no means the only one. Vegetables were also grown in abundance, including beans, peas, lentils, lettuce, and cucumbers. Grapes and fruit trees such as dates, figs, olives, and pomegranates also dotted the river's banks and the delta.

Irrigation of this sort, which depended on the annual flooding, had two major drawbacks. The principal drawback was the occasional failure of the flood to occur. Some years, although it was relatively rare, the rainfall in equatorial Africa was insufficient to produce a good flood for the farmers. On the other hand, there were also occasions when the rainfall produced excessive flooding that prevented farmers from planting and which even washed away their homes and cattle.

The second drawback was that because this form of irrigation harnessed the waters from the annual flood, farmers who used it could still only produce one crop a year. Following the growing and the harvest seasons, the vast fields in the delta and those along the banks of the Nile lay fallow, unusable, until the next flood season arrived six to seven months later. Such a lengthy interval represented a substantial waste: The climate of Egypt was sufficiently warm and sunny to allow two or even three crops a year if only a constant supply of water could be available.

Improving Irrigation

Ancient Egyptians recognized that bringing water to their land year-round was far more desirable than complete dependence on the annual flood. The earliest attempts to utilize the Nile's water during the drought season involved carrying water in clay jars to the fields and dumping it in long furrows dug for irrigation. This process had limited success. It required water carriers to work from sunrise to sunset, and the backbreaking labor could only irrigate relatively small plots of land.

This frieze, or architectural adornment, on an ancient temple portrays Egyptians using shadufs, *devices that enabled them to transfer water from the Nile to their fields.*

Moreover, much of the water was wasted since it evaporated before it ever reached the farmer's field.

Egyptian farmers looked to technology to provide more efficient irrigation techniques. In about 1500 B.C. Egyptians conceived the *shaduf,* a mechanical device consisting of a bucket mounted on a long pole that could be swung around, enabling someone to transfer water from the river into an irrigation ditch. This technique was a vast improvement over carrying water in jars, but a better mechanism, the water wheel, was soon to follow.

The ancient water wheel improved upon the *shaduf.* It was a partly submerged vertical wheel with buckets attached to the rim. As the wheel was rotated, the buckets were filled in the river and then dumped into a trough that carried the water to the fields.

Ancient Water Laws

Given that so much depended on the water supply, use of this precious commodity was closely watched. Although the great annual flood inundated the land along the river, nonetheless, laws regulated the digging of canals, damming of fields, and irrigation of fields during the dry season. Violation of these laws was punishable by death.

The water laws of ancient Egypt were primarily concerned with ensuring that each farmer along the river had fair access to the waters during the floods and that no farmers were denied their fair share of irrigated water. If a farmer, for example, farmed many miles from the river, those owning land close to the river had to allow him to have access to a water canal running through their land.

Water laws also prohibited the taking of water from canals by farmers not contributing to the labor of filling

The *Shaduf*

During the yearly floods of the Nile, water saturated the fields. Once floodwaters receded and the fields dried, however, maximizing crop yields was accomplished by irrigating from wells or canals. A device called a *shaduf* was used to lift the water from the wells or canals and pour it into ditches that carried it to the crops. The *shaduf* is the first-known mechanical device for irrigating fields, and archaeologists believe it was first used around 1500 B.C.

The *shaduf* consists of a long wooden pole balanced across a horizontal support from eight to ten feet above the ground. The beam has a long, thin end and a short, stubby end. From the long end, a ceramic bucket is suspended, and on the short end there is a counterweight of packed dried mud. The farmer pulls on a rope that lowers the long end of the pole, submerging the bucket until it fills with water. He then releases the rope, allowing the counterweight to raise the bucket. He then empties it into a ditch that waters the crops.

If the counterweight of the *shaduf* is the same weight as the filled bucket of water, a worker can irrigate a field all day long without tiring. It is estimated that during droughts, it took about five gallons of water to irrigate ten square feet of land for one day. The *shaduf* is so efficient that it is still used along the Nile in remote areas lacking electricity to run pumps.

the canal with water. How much water one was entitled
to take from a canal depended on how much time one
spent filling that canal. If, for example, ten farmers contributed ten hours of labor filling irrigation canals with
water, any one of them who took more than one hour's
worth of water could be put to death.

For those who paid with their lives for violating water
laws, death did not necessarily end the matter. A person's
behavior while living was believed to affect one's afterlife,
and the gods were thought to take transgressions involving water very seriously. Among the transgressions
believed to affect the afterlife, three pertained to the ethi-
cal use of water; each person hoped that upon passing to
the afterlife he could say, "I have not turned back water
at its springtide [the annual flood] nor stemmed the flow
of running water; I have not broken the channel of a running water; I have never fouled the water, nor have I polluted the land."[4]

Fishing

Whereas people living along the Lower Nile depended on
the floods to water their crops, along the Upper Nile,
where flooding did not occur, people relied much less on
agriculture. Instead, peoples of the Upper Nile praised the
river for its gift of fish and the animals that came to the
banks to drink. Fishing was far more important than
farming to those living along the Upper Nile because the
constant rains that fed the Nile tended to prevent the mat-
uration of grain crops. In order for grain to properly
mature, the roots require alternating periods of wet soil
followed by dry soil. Too much moisture causes root rot
and so kills the plant. People living along the Upper Nile
were able to grow some fruits and vegetables and derived
most of their protein from the plentiful supply of fish.

The most common fish species—and the one most preferred for eating by the peoples along the Upper Nile and
around Lake Victoria—was the Nile perch. Unlike smaller species of perch, these fish grow quickly and can reach

Nilometers

The Egyptians could neither control nor predict the Nile's annual flood, yet they worked to keep track of it each year with the aid of a measurement tool dubbed by modern archaeologists the nilometer. The nilometer was a rudimentary tool used to measure the volume of water flowing through several places on the river during the annual flood.

The most commonly found nilometers were stone pillars erected in the Nile, on which marks were cut, and stone walls along the banks of the river. The builders scratched horizontal marks from top to bottom, one cubit apart. A cubit was a measurement used by the ancient Egyptians that was the distance from a man's elbow to the tip of his index finger—roughly sixteen inches. In the city of Elephantine, the nilometer was a bit different; it was a flight of stone stairs, each stair one cubit high and descending down the bank of the river to the riverbed.

Each year when the floodwaters crested, an appointed person would go to the nilometer and record the high-water mark. Over a period of many years, the inhabitants along the banks of the Nile could determine the amount of water they had received relative to previous years.

Having flood information was valuable. For farmers, the nilometers functioned as simple predictors of the fall harvest; a low nilometer reading below eighteen cubits meant a low crop yield, a very high reading above twenty-two portended excessive flooding and no crop whatsoever, while a medium height reading twenty cubits meant a good crop yield.

Tax collectors also found value in knowing the year's nilometer reading. Just as the farmers could estimate their future crop production, so too could tax collectors estimate how much money the farmers would make.

The nilometer at Elephantine (pictured) consisted of a flight of stairs that measured the height of the river.

four to five feet in length. The combination of size and speed of growth made the Nile perch a major source of food for the Upper Nile. Tilapia, a type of bass, was also plentiful and favored for the firm texture of its meat and its large size. Following these two was the red-tailed Nile catfish. Like other species of catfish, it lives in the mud on the bottom of the Nile and eats things that filter down to the bottom. The catfish was a favorite because a single large fish provided enough meat to feed several families.

Because fish were plentiful, anyone who lived along the Upper Nile could, by flinging wide nets or by dropping a line into the water, feed a family, no matter what the season of the year was. Net fishing was used where the river was slow and calm. Setting out into the river in boats made from bundled papyrus reeds, fishermen would cast a circular net twenty feet in diameter. As it floated down a few feet below the surface, the fisherman would jerk it up by a line tied to his hand and empty the fish into his boat. Archaeologists believe line fishing was also common since they have found ancient bronze hooks that look very much like those used by modern fishermen.

People living along the Lower Nile also fished, even though fish was not as important a part of their diet as it

This relief from a 2200 B.C. tomb shows Egyptians fishing with nets in the Nile.

was for Upper Nile peoples. Along the Lower Nile, fishing required no equipment. People had only to wait for the floods to recede and then pick up the fish stranded in shallow pools. Fish could then be preserved for later by skinning and drying them in the sun or by smoking them in a smokehouse.

Yet even though fish provided valuable nutrition, it was not always utilized. Egyptologists note that during certain periods of Egyptian history, the eating of some species was prohibited among some Nile peoples because they were considered sacred. Any who ate those particular species were viewed as violators of religious law and were considered unclean for having done so. Egyptologists also note that in the ancient Egyptian language, the hieroglyph for the word *detestable* was a fish, suggesting that at one point the prohibition against eating fish was widespread.

Hunting

Ancient civilizations living along the Nile relied on the river to provide other sources of protein as well. The Nile was the home for many fowl and the source of drinking water for a large number of land animals. All along the four-thousand-mile length of the Nile, people knew they could count on the river to attract game that they could kill and eat.

How people went about hunting these animals is well documented. Ancient paintings on tombs depict scenes of people hunting both fowl and larger land animals. The paintings depict aristocrats hunting waterfowl for sport using what archaeologists call a throw-stick, which was a flat piece of wood curved in such a way that a small, sharp projectile could be launched with deadly force. Paintings also depict hunters paddling on the river in papyrus boats approaching flocks of birds and casting nets to capture several of them at once, a method that would have yielded enough meat to feed a family.

Aside from birds, hunters could also capture or kill land animals that came to the river to drink. Especially during times of drought, both large and small animals had to approach the river to quench their thirst. Ancient paintings depict hunters along the banks of the Nile lying in wait of prey. Hunters used bows and arrows, spears, nets, traps, and hunting dogs to bring down prey. Members of the aristocracy could even obtain and train the powerful and swift-footed cheetah to hunt and retrieve game.

In the drier climates along the Lower Nile, the game that approached the river tended to be small desert animals such as rabbits, jackals, large desert lizards such as the river monitor, desert cats, and gazelle. Further upriver in the wetter climates, the game became larger and more dangerous. Paintings have been found depicting hunters in papyrus boats killing wildebeests, crocodiles, and hip-

In this ancient Egyptian engraving, hunters attempt to spear hippopotamuses in the Nile.

popotamuses swimming in the river. Ancient paintings also depict hunters along the river's edge hiding behind rocks and trees and throwing spears at large cats such as lions and cheetahs and hoofed animals such as zebras and wild cattle.

Travel on the Nile

The river's importance for most people along the Nile went far beyond being a source of food, however. The river was also their major transportation route. Caravans of camels and horses transported goods along routes that cut across the Sahara Desert and through the jungles of the Upper Nile basin, but boats of various sizes were used to connect many of the towns along the Nile.

Just how large a boat could be depended on what part of the Nile it was to serve. Along the Lower Nile, from the location of modern-day Aswan to the Mediterranean, boats large enough to carry heavy cargo or many passengers could have been used since this is the only long, continuous stretch that is clear of rapids and cataracts. As the Nile flows through most of Egypt, the slope of the river is so slight that on calm days it provides smooth sailing in both directions.

Boats plying the Lower Nile were aided by the wind. The prevailing winds along this part of the river were southerly, off the Mediterranean, helping boats move against the Nile's current. Although the strength of the winds was not predictable, travelers could at least rely on them to blow nearly every day. Trips south were generally made under full sail in flat-bottom boats that moved with little resistance against the water. Travelers wishing to return home to the north simply took down the sails and drifted with the flow of the Nile.

Just how long the trip took varied with the season. During the annual flood the current was about 6 miles per hour but as slow as 1.5 miles per hour during the drier time of year. Travelers making a long trip, for example

Early Egyptian Boats

The Egyptians pioneered the development of river craft, and there were many different types built for various uses, such as cargo ships to carry agricultural goods, troops, cattle, stone, and even funeral processions. These Egyptian boats were made of both native papyrus and various woods or cedar trees imported from Lebanon.

Papyrus boats were small, so their uses were restricted to hunting or crossing short stretches of water using a paddle or a pole. These boats were made of bundles of bound papyrus reeds lashed together into a long, thin hull in the style of a slight crescent. This lifted the ends out of the water. The bundle was made as wide as possible for stability, and an extra bundle was put on top so that the cargo and crew were kept reasonably dry.

Cedar was very important to the Egyptians as a building material for large boats. These boats were built of relatively short blocks of timber that were braced and secured with rope lashings very much in the same style that was used in papyrus boats. Besides using them for cargo, pharaohs used them as funerary boats that carried them to their final resting places. The world's oldest boat was found in the pyramid of King Khufu, which was completed in 2526 B.C. and measured 150 feet from beam to stern. Most Egyptologists believe it was his funerary barge.

from Thebes north to Memphis, a trip of 550 miles, planned carefully to schedule their trip during the annual flood when the trip would take about eight days. Otherwise, the same trip could take as long as one month when the river was low.

The Nile's value as a major transportation route was, however, confined primarily to Egypt. Although the Nile was the giver of life to all countries through which its waters flowed, it was not a river that facilitated trade, migration, or cultural diffusion between ancient Egypt and the heart of Africa.

Close to the source of the Nile, as the river tumbles out of the highlands of equatorial Africa, it experiences its most dramatic drop in elevation. Between Lake Victoria and the Sudd, for example, the river drops rapidly as it cascades over cataracts and through white-water gorges where large wooden boats would be destroyed and smaller flat-bottom boats and even reed kayaks would easily capsize. As a result, no large freighters or passenger ships traveled the Upper Nile. This area was navigable by small canoelike craft and fishing skiffs, which could be pulled from the river and portaged around cataracts and rapids.

The Nile in Egyptian Religion

The Nile's central role not just in Egypt's trade but also in virtually every aspect of the peoples' lives guaranteed that the river would figure prominently in the religious life of Egypt. Egyptians were polytheists, believers in many gods; not surprisingly, several gods

Two figures of the Nile god Hapi are depicted tying the upper and lower Egyptian kingdoms together in this ancient tomb carving.

were associated with the river. Of these, the two most significant were Hapi and Osiris.

Hapi was the more important of the two gods of the Nile. Painted murals, hieroglyphic inscriptions, and artifacts found in tombs and temples suggest that Egyptians worshiped Hapi even above the sun god, Ra, because without Ra, they could still live—if in darkness—but without Hapi, who controlled the Nile, they would perish. Hapi was responsible for many phenomena associated with water, such as rain and bringing the dew, but most importantly, he brought the annual flood.

Because Egyptians believed Hapi controlled the flowing and flooding of the Nile and the growth of crops, they built temples to him, made sacrifices, and performed rituals to assure the annual flood. According to this cosmological view of the Nile, the river took two forms. One form existed on Earth; it gushed forth each year from somewhere in the depths of the earth to flood the Egyptian valleys and meadows each summer. The other form of the Nile existed in the heavens and provided for the rain that watered the land during the winter and spring.

Osiris was the second major god of the Nile. Like Hapi, Osiris was closely associated with the Nile, but more specifically, he was known for his many achievements of providing water for bountiful harvests and for educating farmers in the use of the river for their crops. For example, many stories are told about Osiris building early canals and mounds to prevent the overflooding of farmlands.

Osiris is represented in paintings as a bearded man wearing white mummy wrappings and sitting on a throne. He wears a red and white crown and holds the symbols of crops, a sheaf of wheat, and supreme power, a staff. His skin is sometimes green to represent vegetation and sometimes red to represent the earth. Osiris's association with water and abundance is revealed in this ancient hymn:

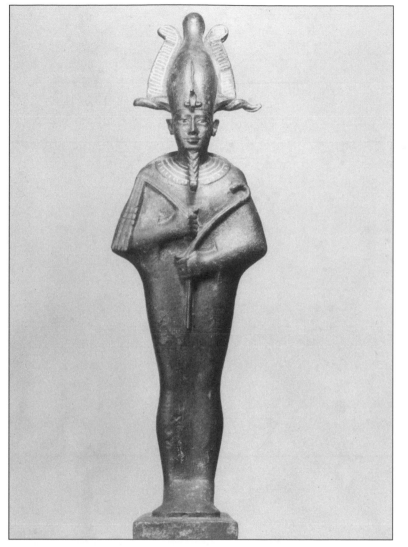

Ancient Egyptians prayed to the god Osiris to provide farmers with water for bountiful crops.

Thou hast made the earth in thy hand, and its waters, and its air, and its green herb, and all its cattle, and all its birds, and all its fishes, and all its reptiles, and [all] its four-footed beasts. . . . He layeth his commands upon men, . . . and the river floods, and the celestial waters, and the staff of life, and every flower . . . he giveth his green herbs; he is the lord of food, he leadeth on abundance, and he giveth it unto all lands.[5]

The overarching theme of the ancient Egyptians' relationship with the Nile was the overwhelming respect they held for the river. That respect was a reflection of a simple appreciation for the water that mysteriously sustained their way of life and their faith that its abundant gift would never cease. The people of ancient Egypt never sought to analyze the river or to change it because it provided them with everything they needed. This relationship was not destined to last forever, as humans sought to bend the river to their will.

3

Harnessing the Nile

Life along the Nile remained relatively unchanged for five thousand years. This was the case not only for the Egyptians but also for all of the other peoples who lived along the Nile from the Sahara Desert south to equatorial Africa. Ancient writings suggest that although the Egyptians were interested in many of nature's marvels, for some reason they were not inclined to probe the mysteries of the Nile. Modern Egyptologists speculate that the Nile was so much a part of ancient Egyptians' everyday lives that it never occurred to them to investigate it in detail.

The task of unraveling the Nile's mysteries—where it came from and why it behaved the way it did—fell to European visitors. As foreign travelers began exploring Egypt around the fifth century B.C., they also marveled at the Nile. But, unlike the Egyptians, they wanted to understand this majestic river, including its source. At first their explorations were driven by nothing more than curiosity, but over time these were driven by an interest in harnessing this seemingly limitless supply of water.

The Search for the Source of the Nile

Around 476 B.C. the first-known European traveler to Egypt, the Greek historian Herodotus, recognized the significance to Egypt of the flooding of the Nile, observing that "Egypt is a gift of the Nile."[6] Herodotus also puzzled over the flooding and the source of the Nile, and he decided to find out how such a vast river could possibly emerge from what appeared to be a stark desert. Herodotus questioned a number of Egyptian priests and other learned individuals about the source but found that none of them knew the answer: "With regard to the source of the Nile, I have found no one among all those with whom I have conversed, whether Egyptians, Libyans, or Greeks, who professed to have any knowledge."[7]

Herodotus set out by boat to find the Nile's source. After journeying for several weeks upriver, he reached the city of Elephantine, where the modern city of Aswan is located. Exhausted and discouraged at not yet reaching the source, he gave up and turned back.

The next recorded attempt to locate the source of the Nile occurred in A.D. 66, when two Roman explorers set sail up the Nile with the intent of finding the source. This was an important issue to the Romans because much of the grain that fed Rome's population came from Egypt, and they wanted to know if they could rely on the river for future crops. Proceeding far beyond Elephantine, the Romans arrived after many months at the Sudd. There, they encountered what they described as an impenetrable swamp that forced them to abandon their quest.

A century following the Roman expedition, the Greek astronomer, mathematician, and geographer Ptolemy drew one of the first maps

Ancient Greek historian Herodotus, the first-known European traveler to Egypt, was unsuccessful in finding the source of the Nile.

of Africa and the Nile, although he never personally mounted an expedition to search for the source. As a result, although his map accurately depicts the Lower Nile as it flows into the Mediterranean, the depiction of the Upper Nile becomes increasingly inaccurate. The map depicts Ptolemy's supposition that the source of the river was two equal-size, perfectly round lakes, side by side; his map places these lakes in what today is Zimbabwe, a thousand miles south of the actual source.

Over the next twelve hundred years or so, explorers continued to search for the Nile's source, and gradually they extended their knowledge of the river. By the fifteenth century, they had accurately identified the two major branches of the Nile, the Blue Nile and the White Nile, and their confluence as they flow north at Khartoum. Still, where those two branches arose remained unknown.

The Industrial Revolution

Exploration aimed at finding the source of the Nile did not really begin in earnest until the late eighteenth century, at the outset of the Industrial Revolution in Europe. At this point, European nations began descending on Africa to capitalize on the untapped natural resources found there. To feed their growing populations and supply their mills, they sought as much wheat and cotton as they could find. In the process, leaders of nations such as Britain and France realized that if they located the source of the Nile, they could better understand the annual flooding and perhaps more efficiently apply the water to increase the production of wheat and cotton.

As part of this effort, in 1858 the British explorer John Speke, working his way up the White Nile, discovered a mammoth lake that the people living there called Ukerewe. Speke renamed it Lake Victoria in honor of England's Queen Victoria, and he declared it to be the source of the Nile.

With the question of the river's source settled, a number of European industrial powers, led by Britain, France, and Belgium, set out to exploit the riches of the Nile. Because these powers focused on wheat and cotton production, the countries of initial interest were those in the hot, dry climates along the Lower Nile: Egypt, Sudan, and Ethiopia.

The European powers, especially Britain, went far beyond simply asking Egypt and its neighbors to increase

In 1853 British explorer John Hanning Speke declared that Lake Victoria was the source of the Nile.

crop production. Europeans—first the French and then the British—sent military expeditions into northern Africa and occupied the region to ensure absolute control over the production of wheat and cotton. By 1882 Britain's military occupied Egypt and Sudan. Although Britain preferred to rule indirectly through Egyptian government officials, British troops saw to it that Britain's interests were put foremost.

Once the British had consolidated their hold on the Lower Nile, they sent engineers and hydrologists to discover how best to harness the Nile's water to increase crop production. With the blessing of Egyptian leaders, British engineers began designing dams to control the annual flooding of the Nile.

For the British, the biggest problem was that the annual flooding of the Nile limited farmers to only a single wheat crop and allowed them to grow barely enough cotton to meet local needs—not enough for export. If Egypt was to produce sufficient cotton to feed Britain's textile mills, more water would be needed and not just for three months a year. To resolve this problem, irrigation projects on a scale unlike anything ever imagined by the ancient Egyptians were designed by British engineers.

Irrigation for year-round crop production required the construction of several dams on the Nile that would fundamentally change the river. Dams would stop the annual flooding by capturing the massive volume of water during the flood season and storing it in reservoirs. The stored water could then be released to the crops as needed during the dry season. In this way, multiple crops of wheat could be grown and high-yield cotton would become a major cash crop.

Damming the Nile

In 1861 engineers completed the first modern irrigation system in the Nile Delta by constructing a series of small dams just north of Cairo that captured part of the annual flood for later use. Buoyed by the success of this project,

The Industrial Revolution in Europe

Many historians consider the European Industrial Revolution to be the most far-reaching influential transformation of human culture since the advent of agriculture eight thousand years earlier.

The Industrial Revolution was a dramatic change in the nature of production: Machines replaced hand tools, steam replaced human or animal power, and skilled craftsmen were replaced by semi-skilled machine operators. The Industrial Revolution resulted in work that had once been performed by individual workers, such as spinning yarn, harvesting crops, milling flour, and transporting goods, being performed with the help of large, powerful steam-driven machines.

Since machines could produce goods such as clothing faster than manual production, industrial nations found that they quickly ran out of all of the cotton they could find in their own countries. To find more cotton, European industrial nations combed the globe, and when they found regions where the climate suited cotton production, they set to work inducing the local farmers to plant it. If necessary, the Europeans altered rivers and lakes to water the crops.

The quest for natural resources such as cotton became so intense that European nations went to war with each other to capture as much farmland as possible in foreign countries. They also went to war against foreign countries to take control of crop production. In some parts of the world, greed on the part of European nations meant using local workers and paying them substandard wages, or, in some cases, using them as slave labor.

the British began building more earthen dams farther south until, in 1909, engineers had constructed the Naj Hammandi Dam, the fifth in a series, five hundred miles south of Cairo. With the completion of each dam, less floodwater inundated the Nile Delta, but more water was available for irrigation during the late annual fall and winter drought.

The system of dams was an unqualified success from nearly everyone's point of view. The dams dramatically increased crop production, pleasing the British, and the farmers along the Nile prospered as well. As this series of earthen dams went up, engineers became increasingly convinced that building a super dam much farther south, one that could store billions of cubic feet of Nile water to irrigate most of Egypt's farmland, was feasible. The site they chose was close to the first cataract near the city of Aswan.

The first phase of the Aswan Dam was completed in 1902 by British engineers and was later enlarged in 1936. This dam, which is 1.25 miles long and stands 126 feet above the river, was, at the time of its completion, the largest dam in the world. To resist the extreme pressure from the water in the massive reservoir, engineers used 780,000 cubic yards of concrete mixed with millions of tons of sand and granite rock. The first year that the reservoir reached its capacity, in 1941, it contained roughly 3 trillion cubic feet of water. To allow boats to navigate on the river, four locks were built on the western side of the dam.

The Aswan Dam, pictured here during the first phase of construction in 1900, provided year-round irrigation for farmers along the Nile and boosted Egypt's agricultural economy.

Prosperity

The harnessing of the Nile with a complex system of dams provided year-round irrigation and propelled the Egyptian agricultural economy beyond those of all of the other Nile countries. Britain and America purchased all of the wheat and cotton that Egyptian farmers could grow, and all involved countries enjoyed the benefits of the harnessing of the Nile.

With the completion of the Aswan Dam, life across Egyptian society improved dramatically. Almost everyone directly or indirectly shared in the new wealth. Money was available for the first time for the construction of schools, fostering the growth of literacy in the country.

The quality of health care also improved dramatically. Money was now available to build urban hospitals and rural clinics. Children received inoculations against common diseases such as measles, cholera, and smallpox that before had killed thousands. Modern sewage systems built with public money reduced illnesses and prolonged lives by improving sanitation.

In addition to water for irrigation, the Aswan Dam provided a source for hydroelectric power. During the first years after completion of the dam, all of the electrical needs of Egypt's capital city, Cairo, and several other large Egyptian cities were fulfilled by power from Aswan. Electricity provided Egypt with the ability to have factories of its own, fostering the growth of a middle class able to enjoy some conveniences such as kitchen appliances and electric lights.

The control of the Nile became the key to Egypt's economic, political, and social stability. As long as none of the countries closer to the source of the Nile interfered with the river's flow, the Egyptian economy would continue to prosper, providing cotton and grain to the industrial giants as well as money and electricity to the Egyptians.

Eventually, Egyptian production of wheat and cotton could not keep up with Britain's ever-increasing demands. British entrepreneurs in alliance with the British government recognized that if damming the Nile within the borders of Egypt could dramatically increase grain and cotton production in that country, similar results might well be achieved closer to the source of the Nile. With that simple premise in mind, the British looked south to Ethiopia and Sudan as the next great sources of cotton and other agricultural products.

An Epidemic of Dams

The two major trunks of the Nile south of Khartoum, the Blue Nile and the White Nile, could potentially water tens of thousands of additional square miles of crops if, like the Lower Nile, they were dammed. In 1925 the British built the first dam on the Blue Nile with a reservoir capacity of 27 billion cubic feet. Twelve years later the White Nile had its first dam with a capacity 2.5 times that of the Blue Nile dam. Within the next two decades two more major dams appeared on the White Nile in Sudan. In later decades, primarily during the 1960s, more dams were added to both rivers.

The damming of the Nile upriver from Egypt did not bode well for the country's water supply and economy. The dams south of Egypt were suddenly snaring a large share of the annual floodwaters, meaning that Egyptian reservoirs were no longer filling to capacity during the flood season. This disturbing development meant that during the dry season, the amount of water in the Egyptian reservoirs was no longer sufficient to satisfy the needs of the nation's farmers.

Desperate to remedy this unforeseen problem, the Egyptian government petitioned the British to cease building any more dams in Sudan or Ethiopia and to restrict the amount of water that could be captured in reservoirs south of the Aswan Dam. The British, however, who politically and economically controlled all three countries,

The British built the
Sennar Dam in 1935
to control the waters
of the Blue Nile.

and whose interests were best served by building more
dams, turned a deaf ear to the Egyptian complaints.

Contributing to the problem of a reduced water supply was a burgeoning demand for water upriver.
Prosperity had now arrived in Sudan and Ethiopia, just
as it had decades earlier in Egypt. The farmers of these
two previously impoverished nations began to enjoy
better sanitation, an improved medical system, and
higher quality nutrition. All of these improvements

resulted in a sudden surge in population. As the populations of these countries ballooned, so too did the demand for water.

Further complicating the water problem on the Nile was the fact that the country to feel the loss of water more than any other was the country that used the most water but contributed the least, Egypt. Daniel Hillel, professor of soil physics and hydrology at the University of Massachusetts, makes this observation:

Growing Friction over Water

Because the Nile is the lifeline of northeastern Africa, threats to its continued flow have caused friction to surface first between Egypt and Sudan and later between all ten countries that share the Nile. Although most of the countries in the Nile basin do not have the infrastructure in place to make greater use of the Nile's waters, a conflict is brewing between those countries that want to use more of it.

Currently, Egypt and Sudan consume 90 percent of the Nile's water, an amount that was settled upon in the 1959 Agreement for the Full Utilization of the Nile Waters. Egypt, however, takes the lion's share of this ration, using 55 billion cubic meters of water to Sudan's 18 billion. By comparison, Ethiopia uses less than 1 percent of all Nile water, even though a significant percent of the river's water originates in Ethiopia.

Ethiopians are now talking for the first time about irrigating their desert for agriculture, just as the Egyptians are doing. If they do, they will take millions of gallons a day away from the flow into Egypt. Government officials in Ethiopia and Sudan have made it clear that they plan to develop irrigation networks and plumbing systems, making more use of the Nile waters. At the same time, Egypt is beginning to demand more and more water.

As a result, the debates surrounding water usage are getting more and more tense. The Egyptian, Sudanese, and Ethiopian governments met to discuss water allocation several times in 2001. Still, with an army of four hundred thousand soldiers and the most modern weapons, Egypt has the muscle to potentially use force to defend this precious commodity.

The pattern of water demand and use in the Nile basin contrasts sharply with the pattern of supply. The paradox is that the countries contributing the most water are using the least, and vice versa. The humid equatorial zones [at the source] use little of the river's water because their humid climate makes irrigation less necessary. . . . Sudan . . . Ethiopia, . . . and Egypt are all principal users of the water but . . . contribute little or none at all.[8]

By the late 1950s the Egyptians recognized that they would somehow have to assure themselves of a water supply that did not rely on the annual flood, even if their upriver neighbors further decreased the volume of water flowing into Egypt. The answer was to build yet another, much larger, dam.

The Aswan High Dam

During the late 1950s Egypt's president, Gamal Abdel Nasser, declared the need to build a super dam called the Aswan High Dam (in Arabic, Sadd al-Ali) just a few miles south of the existing Aswan Dam. Nasser said the dam was necessary to more effectively control the annual flooding, to store a greater volume of water from each annual flood for use during the dry season, and to generate more hydroelectric power. Although the first Aswan Dam already provided these three benefits, Nasser contended that without the super dam, Egypt's economic future was threatened.

Everyone understood that the new dam would lessen Egyptian dependence on its upriver neighbors because it would create an immense reservoir capable of storing many years of floodwater. Nasser alluded to the competing demands for the Nile's water when he said, "After completion of the High Dam, Egypt will no longer be the historic hostage of the upper partners to the Nile basin."[9]

Britain and the United States initially agreed to finance building the dam, but then withdrew their support for the project. In the absence of support from these Western powers, Nasser turned to the Soviet Union for help. Hoping to gain influence in a strategically crucial region of the world, the Soviets gladly agreed to build and finance the project for Egypt. Four hundred Soviet engineers arrived in Egypt to design and construct the new dam. As part of the construction, twelve electricity-generating turbines were installed capable of generating twenty-one hundred megawatts of electricity.

The Benefits of the Aswan High Dam

By 1971, when the reservoir it created had filled, the Aswan High Dam became the backbone of the Egyptian

The Aswan High Dam was built during the 1960s to create a reservoir capable of storing many years of floodwater.

The Aswan High Dam

Construction of the Aswan High Dam began in January 1960, four miles south of the old Aswan Dam. The site was chosen for its granite bedrock, which was needed to support the massive weight of the stone, sand, and concrete. Constructed by Russian engineers, this type of dam is called a gravity dam because it depends on gravity to keep it in place. It is designed so that the sheer weight of the dam keeps it from sliding or being overturned by the pressure of the water. The first phase was completed in 1964 and the final stage in 1970, costing more than $1 billion.

The dam is a rubble-filled structure, made from several layers of packed sand, gravel, dirt, and granite rubble. The bulk of materials used in building the Aswan High Dam is the granite; the amount used is estimated to be about seventeen times the amount used to build the great Giza pyramid. Once this mass was in place, it was encased in an outer shell consisting of 56,242 cubic yards of concrete.

The dam is the shape of an inverted pyramid, narrow at the bottom and wide at the top. At the dam site the Nile is 1,800 feet wide and the concrete dam itself extends deep into each bank, making it more than 3,000 feet long at its base and 11,000 feet across the top, which rises 365 feet above the river.

The reservoir that trails behind the dam is named Lake Nasser in honor of the Egyptian president Gamal Abdel Nasser. It holds the world record for reservoirs, holding 5.9 trillion cubic feet of water, an average volume of discharge at 3,616 cubic yards per second and a maximum of 16,172 cubic yards per second, and twelve power-generating units that provide over 2,100 megawatts of electric power.

economy. The colossal dam increased Egypt's cultivatable land by 30 percent, doubled the country's electrical power generating capacity, and created a reservoir large enough to absorb the worst possible flood while it stored enough water to supply the nation through several years of drought. The reservoir, known in Egypt as Lake Nasser, became the world's largest man-made lake.

The Aswan High Dam's value to Egypt has been documented in many ways, one of which has been the five times it has saved Egypt from potentially disastrous floods: in 1964—while still under construction—1975, 1988, 1998, and 1999. Another value has been the amount of electricity generated, which Egypt would otherwise have needed to purchase.

The Aswan High Dam's effect that Egyptians are most proud of, however, is the blooming of the Egyptian desert. The increased volume of stored water has permitted the growing of three crops a year on millions of acres that before could produce only one crop. Of even greater pride is that millions of acres of desert have been converted into productive farmland.

The Aswan High Dam, shown here during construction in 1964, has enabled Egyptians to convert millions of acres of desert into productive farmland.

Tourism on the Nile

The Aswan High Dam has also provided one unexpected benefit to the people of Aswan. Once the lake filled, entrepreneurs realized its value as a recreational area and as a cultural attraction for tourists interested in Egyptian archaeology. Although the Nile had provided opportunities for leisurely boat trips for thousands of years, tourism took a huge jump following the construction of the Aswan High Dam and the creation of Lake Nasser. This enormous lake provides tourists with many recreational and cultural activities that have contributed millions of dollars to the local economy. The central attractions are recreational boating and fishing and cruise boats that provide multiday trips around the lake, stopping at the sites of several ancient Egyptian temples.

This satellite image reveals the enormity of the reservoir, known as Lake Nasser, created by the Aswan High Dam.

Since the lake's creation, hotels, campgrounds, restaurants, boating facilities, and other concessions have served the needs of the tourists. Just how much tourists contribute to the local economies is uncertain, but local civic leaders view the surge in tourism as another benefit of the massive dam.

Environmentalists and biologists, on the other hand, are not happy about the lake's popularity as a recreational attraction. Scientists concerned with the health of the Nile view the tourists, cruise boats, hotels, and many industries that have sprung up along the river's banks as sources of pollution. As the twenty-first century begins, there is increasing evidence that the world's longest and most famous river is suffering as a result of irresponsible development.

4
. . . .

The Suffering Nile

Modifying the natural flow of the Nile, principally in the form of damming the river, has dramatically altered the Lower Nile basin with the result that crop yields are dropping, water quality is declining, and plant and animal life in the river is suffering. The Upper Nile, although relatively unaffected by damming, has its own set of problems. Industrial pollutants have contaminated the water, and the introduction of invasive species to the river has been responsible for disease and death to humans as well as to indigenous wildlife populations.

The Tragedy of Dams

Some of the environmental problems associated with damming a river were known at the time the first Nile dams were built during the mid–nineteenth century. The British builders of the dams, however, along with Egyptian government officials, chose to overlook the long-term problems in favor of the short-term gains to be made by increasing cotton and grain production.

By the mid–twentieth century, agronomists and hydrologists began to see the negative effects of altering the natural flow of the Nile. Although subtle at first, signs of ill health began to appear, indicating the benefits of damming the river were in decline. Moreover, there were signs that the benefits that had been realized might soon entirely reverse themselves, leaving the Lower Nile in worse condition than had been the case before the building of the dams.

Fish Versus Dams

Dams create imposing obstacles to the natural movement of river fish. The many large dams that now span the Nile have impeded fish from migrating up and down the river. During the initial construction and filling of a dam, river habitat is lost while reservoir habitat is created. This conversion from river to reservoir has been detrimental to many species, causing them to die from starvation, changes in water temperature, changes in water quality, and loss of mature spawning habitat.

Many dams rely on storage of water during high flow periods for use later in the year during droughts. This alteration of the natural river cycle can impact habitat availability and stability during periods of spawning and incubation. Determining appropriate flows for maintenance of habitat during all life phases is an important step in defining bounds on dam operations. Problems arise when the need to release water from the dams for human consumption is in conflict with the needs of the fish to migrate and spawn.

Another major problem for migrating fish is the need for large hydroelectric dams to drop a large proportion of the river through turbines that generate electricity. Large quantities of fish trying to migrate downriver enter the generating flow and are liquefied by the spinning turbine blades. Much research has been done to minimize this destruction to fish, such as placing fish screens at turbine inlets as well as bubble curtains, acoustic barriers, electrical fields, and underwater lights.

The result of large dams on the Nile is that the numbers of migratory fish have dropped significantly since the construction of the major dams. Attempts to assist the fish have provided some small improvements, but environmentalists and the fishing industry abhor the destruction of fish stocks that results from the damming of the Nile.

Although the damming of the Nile had finally controlled the flooding of the northern section of the river, provided water for crops during the dry season, and generated hydroelectricity for millions of people, the waters of the Nile had changed. They now lacked much of the nutrients that had once been present, and without them crop yields were declining—one unmistakable indication that something was very wrong.

The Loss of the Annual Flood

From the standpoint of the farmers along the Nile, the most serious consequence of controlling the annual flood is what agronomists call siltation, the accumulation of silt in reservoirs. Before the building of the dams, the Nile carried silt—a natural fertilized soil made up of minerals and organic material—along with the water. During the great annual flood, the river deposited an estimated 4 million tons of silt annually along the flooded banks and on the Nile Delta, where it nourished the crops. Where the river is dammed, the silt is trapped at the bottom of the many reservoirs and no longer reaches the crops.

The Aswan High Dam, for example, traps 98 percent of the silt that travels down the Nile from Ethiopia. Since thousands of tons of silt are no longer annually deposited in the delta, the farmland's fertility is diminishing. In response, farmers have been forced to use more than a million tons of synthetic fertilizer annually as a substitute for the natural nutrients that no longer arrive as part of an annual flood. For several reasons, artificial fertilizers are a poor substitute for the nutrients the Nile once provided: They are unaffordable for many farmers, are difficult to use properly, and have many detrimental effects on peoples' health.

The silt that no longer reaches the farmers' fields does not disappear, however. Instead, it accumulates in the reservoirs. As silt settles to the bottom over many years, it displaces water, thereby diminishing the capacity of reservoirs. Hydrologists refer to the accumulation of silt in

reservoirs as dead volume. As this dead volume increases, reservoirs gradually lose their ability to control flooding and to provide adequate water for irrigation—negating the very reasons for their construction. Removing this accumulated silt is a huge job in the smaller reservoirs. Worse, siltation in large reservoirs such as Lake Nasser is irreversible. According to engineers at Columbia University studying the Aswan High Dam siltation problem, "The quantities of sediments which will accumulate in Lake Nasser are so large that there are no plausible ways to remove them in the future."[10]

The Nile dams also have the detrimental effect of increasing the salinity of the soil. Salt has always been one of the many minerals suspended in the water of the river. As irrigated soil dries, salt is left behind. Over time, the salt content can accumulate to the point where it poisons the plants. Prior to the construction of the dams, when the Nile annually flooded the farmlands, the huge gush of water washed away the salt content in a process called

A Nile basin farmer stands in his field. The construction of dams along the Nile has prevented soil-enriching silt from reaching his farmland.

leaching, which prevented harmful salt concentrations. In the absence of the floods, salt continues to build up, reducing the productivity of the soil.

Ironically, even though damming stores water, most reservoirs actually decrease the annual volume of available water. The huge, expansive lakes that trail behind dams expose thousands of square miles of surface water to the hot sun, far more exposure than happens in the narrow natural river. The greater the exposed surface area, the more water that is lost to evaporation. Lake Nasser, for example, the huge lake behind the Aswan High Dam, loses to evaporation between 270 and 450 billion cubic feet of water annually. This loss represents a significant percent of Egypt's Nile water.

Another reason hydrologists point out that dams are of limited use is water loss due to seepage. None of the dams on the Nile is 100 percent concrete. All of them are called embankment dams, and they are principally made of mounded earth, sand, and rock held in place by a coating of concrete. The Aswan High Dam, for example, uses millions of tons of large porous stones and sand. Consequently, water loss through seepage is significant.

Because much of the Aswan High Dam is constructed from porous materials, water loss through seepage is significant.

Many of these problems were foreseeable, but in the case of the Aswan High Dam, they were ignored. Daniel Hillel makes this overriding comment on the environmental consequences of the Aswan High Dam: "The succession of events leading to the construction of the High Dam provides an instructive tale of intertwined power politics, personal ambition, national pride, and rivalry over resources, in face of which all considerations of ultimate environmental consequences were largely ignored."[11]

The Mediterranean

The consequences go well beyond declining agricultural yields, however. For millions of years the Nile has played a significant role in the ecology of the eastern Mediterranean Sea. Before the 1970s the annual flooding of the delta released tons of organic nutrients into the waters off the coast of Egypt, which fed small fish and marine invertebrate populations. When the dams ended the annual flood of silt and nutrients, the commercial fishermen noticed a sudden significant decline in their catch. The average catch off the coast of Egypt declined from nearly thirty-five thousand tons in 1962 and 1963 to less than one-fourth of this tonnage following the construction of the Aswan High Dam. Even the shrimp catch in the Mediterranean has decreased due to the change in the Nile flow. Biologists emphasize the damaging effect of the dams by reporting,

> Before the High Dam was built, fifty percent of the Nile flow drained into the Mediterranean. During an average flood, the total discharge of nutrient salts was estimated to be approximately 5,500 tons of phosphate and 280,000 tons of silicate. The nutrient-rich flood water, or Nile Stream, was approximately fifteen kilometers [9.3 miles] wide and had sharp boundaries. . . . These sediments are now trapped behind the dam.[12]

Egypt's Achilles Heel

There is always an inherent danger with dams because once they are filled, they present their builders with the potential of massive destruction should they catastrophically fail. In this sense, the Aswan High Dam has become Egypt's Achilles heel.

In 1973 German writer and engineer Michael Heim published his novel Aswan, *in which he explores the potential for disaster. Heim consulted with dam engineers, hydrologists, and seismologists for his research into the weaknesses of the dam. Were the dam to fail, Heim believes the following scenario might occur as the water surges toward the sea.*

A surge of 164 billion cubic meters [241.5 billion cubic yards] of water bursts through the 100-meter-high [325 feet] walls of a dam, emptying its 500-kilometer-long [310 miles] reservoir in one catastrophic instance. A city three kilometers downstream is rocked by a gale-force wind similar to that preceding a tsunami. Seconds later a 30-meter-high [97 feet] wall of water barrels through, toppling buildings as tall as 10 stories. The head of the flood continues pulsing toward the sea, streaming for the capital city [Cairo] of 15 million people. It reaches the capital on the sixth day, traveling at 30 kilometers [18.5 miles] an hour. The streets are inundated; water reaches 15 meters high.

The Mediterranean was particularly vulnerable to this choking off of waterborne nutrients. In marked contrast to more fertile, nutrient-rich seas such as the North Sea and the Arabian Sea, the Mediterranean is noted for its nutrient-poor waters, which contribute to its low fish populations. According to biology professors Sayed El-Sayed and Gert L. van Dijken at Texas A&M University, "Since 1965 when the [Aswan] High Dam became fully operational, the Nile flow to the Mediterranean has greatly diminished. The decrease in fertility of the southeastern Mediterranean waters caused by the High Dam has had a catastrophic effect on marine fisheries."[13]

Cultural Displacement

The construction of giant dams has harmed more than the natural environment. Each dam displaced people living on the lands flooded by its reservoir. Planning each dam raised the thorny problem of uprooting and resettling people whose families and tribes had occupied these lands as far back as the pharaohs. Those evicted by a dam were often forced to move to land of poorer quality or unsuited to their traditional lifestyles. Those forced to move were also frequently from ethnic groups that had already been excluded from the process of planning for the dams.

Along with the people displaced by the flood were archaeological sites and cultural relics. Ancient temples, tombs, and priceless artifacts had to be moved or lost beneath billions of gallons of reservoir water. The cost to move these huge edifices and artifacts meant that decisions had to be made to determine which would be saved and which would be forever lost. The United Nations organized an international project to save some of the more important temples and monuments.

One site saved from the waters of Lake Nasser was the temple of Abu Simbel, which cost $40 million and took four years to save. Abu Simbel has two temples built by Ramses II, who lived between 1279 and 1213 B.C. Four sixty-five-foot-tall statues of Ramses sit in pairs flanking the entrance. This temple was rescued from a watery grave by cutting it into 1,423 blocks, which were removed and reassembled on higher land. Many other temples, however, were left to lie forever beneath the rising waters of Lake Nasser.

The Pollution of the Nile

Unlike the problems caused by the dams on the Lower Nile, the Upper Nile suffers from water pollution. The Upper Nile nations of Rwanda, Burundi, Tanzania, and Uganda are among the poorest in the world. Desperate to provide jobs for their people, these countries have allowed thousands of unregulated small factories to discharge

Workers rescue the temple of Abu Simbel, which was due to be flooded by the creation of Lake Nasser.

their various wastes directly into the Nile. At the same time, the growing populations of these countries have created towns and villages along the Nile that lack modern sanitary facilities. As a consequence, tons of garbage and human waste flow into the Upper Nile, poisoning both people and wildlife.

The volume of waste is substantial. The minister of public works and water resources for Egypt, Mahmoud Abu Zeid, said regarding the use of the Nile as a sewer, "A survey of waste water discharged in the Nile revealed 5.4 billion cubic metres [7 billion cubic yards] annually of both sewage and industrial waste water, of which 2.2 billion is partially treated sewage water and 3.2 billion is industrial waste mixed with sewage water."[14]

Pollution has raised doubts about the quality and safety of the fishing industry. Although the Nile inevitably received some waste during the time of the pharaohs, the tonnage of impurities dumped in the river today is far more damaging. Annually, thousands of tons of fish are caught for local and foreign consumption from Lake Victoria and the Upper Nile. Despite the considerable investment to upgrade and modernize fish processing plants, there is still concern about the healthfulness of the fish. For example, veterinary authorities in Spain and Italy have detected an unacceptable level of bacteriological contamination in fish from Tanzania, Rwanda, and Burundi. As a

Illness from Pollution of the Nile

The extent of human illness from the pollution of the Nile is more extreme than most people realize. Many poor workers whose drinking water comes from the Nile without purification suffer illness associated with poisoning. The leading serious illness is kidney failure.

According to Yomna Kamel in the September 10, 1999, issue of the *Middle East Times,* "Dr. Abdel Rahman Al Refaai, head of Internal Medicine Unit at the local hospital reports that more than half of patients treated at the hospital's Internal Medicine Unit suffer liver and kidney diseases and infections. It is all because of the polluted water they drink." Dr. Refaai adds "I don't drink water directly from the tap and I advise people either to drink mineral water or use a water purifier. Unfortunately, most people cannot afford to buy water filters and purifiers. They are villagers and laborers working for furniture workshops."

Research on liver diseases, which was carried out ten years ago by Refaai, showed that around 25 percent of all people drinking the Nile's water suffer from liver ailments mostly due to water pollution. This pollution is at its worst where it accumulates from various dumping sites. River pollution includes municipal wastewater, industrial toxins, and household rubbish that find their way directly to the river.

result, in March 1997 the European Commission, a European committee reviewing complaints about imports, announced that all Nile perch imported from the Upper Nile must be subject to a bacteriological examination for salmonella and other pathogens upon entry to Europe.

Pollution has also reduced demand for fish at home. Omayma Ahmed, a housewife living near Lake Victoria, reports to a newspaper reporter,

> We stopped eating Nile fish like catfish and bolti. Although bolti, locally known as the shabar, is our popular dish, we cannot eat it anymore. A kind of worm lives in shabar's gills and cooking does not kill them. Only visitors and poor people eat the shabar these days simply because they do not know it is polluted.[15]

Pollution associated with the timber industry has also contributed to the problems of the fishing industry. Deforestation of the regions around the lake—the result of woodcutting to provide domestic cooking fuel—increases topsoil erosion and silting in the lake. In recent years this flow of nutrient-laden soil into the lake has caused an explosion of water hyacinth and algae blooms, which exhaust the oxygen in the water, causing fish to die. Environmental pressures on Lake Victoria are tremendous, and thus far all efforts to manage them have proved fruitless.

Tourism in the Upper Nile region further contributes to the pollution. Hotels along the banks of the river as well as hundreds of floating hotels dump their waste in the river, and even though they are required to treat the refuse before its discharge, bacteria such as E. coli find their way into the lake. Pollution laws are rarely effective, especially in poor countries, because lacking money to construct sewage treatment plants, these nations lack the infrastructure that makes compliance possible.

Population Pressure

Underlying all the problems besetting the Nile, the governments that profited from the natural resources of the river failed to anticipate the population explosion that occurred during the twentieth century. The surge in population, which occurred along both the Upper and Lower Nile, was the result of the construction of the many dams and the thousands of industries that sprang up along the banks of the river. The dams and industrial development created wealth. But the increased food production and improved standard of living that accompanied it meant that all along the Nile populations also began to grow for the first time in thousands of years.

Ballooning populations along the Nile are demanding more of the river's water for drinking, sanitation, washing clothes, and industrial use. All of these demands, which were relatively benign one hundred years ago, are today reducing the water available for agriculture in the Lower Nile and are poisoning the fish populations along the entire length of the river.

Tourism and exploding populations along the Nile have contributed to pollution and increased demand for the river's water.

Water consumption in modern cities fluctuates considerably, but conservative estimates of average use for city dwellers is roughly 400 cubic feet per month, which equates to about 3,000 gallons. If this rough estimate is then applied to the present population of Egypt, the annual consumption would be 312 billion cubic feet. When the annual consumption of the populations of Sudan and Ethiopia are factored in, 60 million and 35 million people, respectively, the annual consumption is just under 1 trillion cubic feet—a significant loss of water that would otherwise be available for farmers.

The population growth that has led to increased demand for water is comparatively recent. Egyptologists estimate that the population of Egypt during the Old Kingdom (2625–2130 B.C.) was 2 million. More than a thousand years later, at the end of the New Kingdom in 1075 B.C. the population had only increased by 0.5 million to about 3 million people. By the beginning of the

People in large cities like Cairo (pictured) compete with agriculture for water from the Nile.

nineteenth century, three thousand years later, the population had grown to 4.3 million. During this period of nearly forty-five hundred years, before any dam or industrial construction on the Nile, Egypt's population increased by 2.3 million people, an average annual increase of just 511 people.

Following the building of many of the first dams by the British during the nineteenth century, however, Egypt's population exploded. At the end of the nineteenth century, the country's population had grown to 10 million, an average annual increase of 57,000. Following the building of the Aswan Dam, the population surged to 26 million in 1960, an average annual increase of roughly 267,000 people; today, after the construction of the Aswan High Dam, the population stands at 65 million, an average annual increase over the past forty-two years of just under 930,000 people.

The population trends for the other Nile countries are similar although not as dramatic. Nonetheless, this population surge creates significant competition with agriculture for the precious water of the Nile along the Lower Nile and for clean water along the Upper Nile.

Disruptions to the Nile Biosystem

The changes to the Nile's flow and the pollution of its water have created a river the ancient Egyptians would not recognize and have altered a habitat that evolved over tens of thousands of years. The ecological ill health of Lake Victoria and the Upper Nile has already caused the extinction of many fish species. One example of this phenomenon is what has happened to a family of fish called the cichlids. Lake Victoria was home to as many as four hundred species of cichlids, making it one of the most species-diverse lakes in the world. However, the number of cichlid species has suddenly plunged to two hundred because a disruption in the food chain has caused the larger Nile perch to switch from eating other food fish to eating cichlids. Les Kauffman, a chief scientist at Boston

University, characterizes this loss of half the cichlid species as "the greatest vertebrate mass extinction in recorded history."[16]

The ecological imbalance has also struck the plant life of the Nile. Pollution of the river has killed several fish species that kept plant populations in check, resulting in the prolific growth of plants such as algae and the water hyacinth, which now spread throughout the Upper Nile and across Lake Victoria. As these plants spread, they consume nutrients and oxygen while blocking sunlight needed by plants living at greater depths. Massive die-offs of plants occur, which further deplete oxygen in the water.

The Nile and the people living along the river are suffering from a variety of consequences resulting from human-inflicted alterations to the river since the middle of the nineteenth century. During the 1980s and 1990s, as the health of the river declined, members of the international scientific community began to coordinate their research with the governments along the Nile to find solutions to the ills of the river. Fortunately for everyone, steps are now being taken that suggest there is hope for the Nile.

5

Hope and the Nile

Caring for the Nile so it can serve future generations requires addressing the political, economic, and social needs of those who depend on its water today without placing further strain on the river itself. To achieve these objectives, local and international agencies are now focusing on long-term solutions to the problems stemming from the damming of the river and the unregulated industries poisoning the river's waters and wildlife.

Hope for the Nile also rests on repairing the damage that has already been inflicted on the river. Especially for the Lower Nile, the single factor that is linked to more problems than any other is the series of dams built since the mid-1800s. The second most destructive factor has been the use of the Nile as a sewer for industrial toxins and human waste from a ballooning population living along its banks.

Solving the problems of the Nile, however, involves more than dealing with dams and pollutants. The problems have been compounded by the inability of the ten African countries that border the Nile to agree on how to utilize its water. Since the middle of the twentieth century, the Nile basin has been a place of dispute and even occasional warfare over rights to the water and changes made to its natural flow. Very often, a change in the river enhances one country's water supply while diminishing that of another. Diplomats have coined the word *hydropolitics* to describe the political problems associated with a river that passes through many countries, many of which have divergent views on how the river should be used and how the water should be apportioned.

Rethinking the Nile Dams

All scientists, engineers, and politicians who have studied the dams on the Nile readily agree on two points: First, the dams are at the heart of many of the Nile's problems, and second, removing them in hopes of restoring the river to its previous health is impossible. Removing dams is not an option, if for no other reason than the hydroelectricity these dams generate supplies up to 50 percent of the electricity needs of those living along the Nile. Given this dilemma, scientists have focused their attention on the specific problems caused by dams in an attempt to improve the design of future dams and to retrofit existing dams to reduce their adverse environmental effects.

Mahmoud Abu Zeid, Egypt's minister of irrigation and water resources, and other Egyptian government officials extolled the many benefits of the Aswan High Dam. However, Zeid concedes that the long-term effects of the dam were not taken into consideration at the time the dam was constructed. In 1999 Zeid commented, "There have been concerns that insufficient consideration as to who ultimately benefits and who ultimately pays for dams went into the decision-making process."[17]

New Dams

Civil engineers recognize the need to improve the design of dams to remedy the many problems caused by large dams. Because of their massive size, their adverse environmental impact in the form of siltation, evaporation,

and harm to migrating fish is similarly enormous. The answer, some engineers and policy makers say, is to build more, smaller dams.

Hydroelectric dams along the Nile generate electricity for cities such as Cairo (pictured).

One alternative to giant dams such as the Aswan High Dam is called the check dam. These earthen dams are small and are built on shallow tributaries to provide flood control and water storage. The small dams contain excess water flow in a small reservoir behind the structure during the flood season. Pressure created in the reservoir area helps force the stored water into the ground, thereby replenishing nearby groundwater reserves. The water stored behind the dam is primarily used for irrigation during the dry season, but it can also be used for livestock and domestic needs. The problem of siltation is resolved by completely opening the dams before they dry up, allowing all silt to flow to irrigated fields. Because check dams are small, they can be built just about anywhere, unlike giant dams. Consequently, they can easily be built in areas where the reservoir is deep and narrow, thereby reducing water loss due to evaporation, which is a serious drawback at the two larger Aswan dams.

Check Dams

Many hydrologists and environmentalists believe that water scarcity caused by population pressures, deforestation, soil erosion, and rising industrial demand means that a severe water shortage is looming along the Lower Nile. Given the nature of rainfall in equatorial Africa, many believe one of the solutions to meeting the growing demand for water for domestic and agricultural use is to construct more small check dams and fewer giant dams.

Despite having a centuries-old tradition of using innovative small-scale water irrigation structures, Egypt and Sudan have turned away from many of its indigenous technologies in recent decades in favor of imported modern technologies, such as large-scale dam and canal systems, electric or diesel lift irrigation, and drip and sprinkler systems.

Compared with large-scale, high-tech approaches to water management, check dams appear to be a more appropriate technology for poor rural areas. For example, in contrast to modern large dam projects, check dams are a lower cost and a less environmentally and socially disruptive alternative for irrigation. Check dams do not submerge large tracts of land or alter river courses. In contrast to large dams and other modern technology, check dams require very little skilled labor and few financial resources to build and maintain them. For these reasons, they are more affordable to poor nations. The initial investment made can usually be recovered in one or two seasons through the ensuing increases in agricultural production.

From an environmental perspective, small-scale structures such as check dams also seem to be the best choice for several reasons. First, they are a more efficient reservoir system than large dams; second, they help to counter some of the adverse effects of the flood season by allowing more percolation of water into the soil; and third, since these water sources are smaller and locally based, they are more easily modified to meet the needs of individual farmers than large dams.

The problem with the check dams, however, is their inability to generate electricity, a major objective of dam construction. Water must cascade at least one hundred feet and in very large volumes to efficiently spin the turbines that generate electricity. Thus, hydroelectricity can only be generated in large dams.

For civil engineers, the problem remains to design dams capable of generating hydroelectricity while minimizing the siltation and evaporation problems. Engineers have designed dams that reduce the siltation problem by constructing massive sluice gates built near the bottom of the dams. Whenever siltation begins to occur, the sluice gates can be opened to flush the silt from the bottoms of the reservoirs in one single, massive eruption of water. Such a system has two benefits: The reservoir is purged of silt, and crops downriver receive the nutrient-rich silt in a controlled flood. Dam engineers believe that the result will be reservoirs without dead volume.

Planners are addressing the loss of water to evaporation by placing dams in cooler climates and by selecting sites that create deep reservoirs with small surface areas. Dam engineers contend that a tall dam allowing for the cascading of a large volume of water capable of spinning hydroelectric turbines need not involve a large reservoir of water exposed to the evaporation of the sun. As an example, a dam currently under construction at Bujagali in Uganda, which will be built solely for hydroelectricity, will generate 250 megawatts but will have a reservoir of only 1.5 square miles. This compares very favorably with the Aswan High Dam, which generates 2,100 megawatts but has an enormous 3,000-square-mile reservoir.

Solving Water Shortages

Even if evaporation problems can be solved, the fact remains that water is a scarce commodity along the Lower Nile. In spite of the massive flow of the river, it is the only renewable and reliable source of water for

Egypt, Sudan, and Ethiopia. Since the 1950s, as the populations of these countries have increased astronomically, the Nile has been unable to satisfy the water requirements of these nations. To make matters worse, their needs will increase as populations rise, industrial

The Pros and Cons of the Bujagali Dam

In 1996 the government of Uganda approached a major construction company to build a hydroelectric dam on the Nile that would be 100 feet tall and would generate 250 megawatts of electricity to meet the growing needs of the Ugandan people. After five years of research, planning, and design, the dam is finally under construction.

Those supporting the dam see advantages that will directly flow from the availability of adequate electrical power. They also see this dam as the only way to introduce computer technology to this poor country that will enable Uganda's next generation to learn in an environment powered by electricity. Ugandan workers, who currently find themselves out of work ninety days per year due to blackouts, will enjoy more income stability. Many also hope that the electricity generated from the dam will help local medical facilities that are presently at the mercy of power shortages in saving lives and preserving temperature-sensitive children's vaccines.

Not everyone, however, believes the dam is a good idea. Opponents of the Bujagali Dam point to an estimated loss of income to about sixty-eight hundred people who will lose income from their farmland, the harm to local fish stocks, the submersion of highly productive agricultural land on the river's banks, and the loss of biodiversity due to changes to spawning grounds for river animals. In addition, dam opponents believe it will increase serious water-borne diseases like malaria and schistosomiasis, a disease carried by parasitic worms that causes serious blood problems. Stagnant pools of water are breeding grounds for malaria-carrying mosquitoes and schistosomiasis-spreading water snails. Malaria is already a leading cause of death in Uganda.

The project will also drown Bujagali Falls, a spectacular series of cascading rapids, which Ugandans consider a national treasure. Opponents also believe that tourism around Bujagali Falls will disappear because the dam will prevent rafters and fishermen from enjoying the natural cascades.

growth takes place, and more land is irrigated with Nile water to feed their growing populations.

In the late 1970s Egyptian leaders began to come to grips with the fact that there was no other source of water than the Nile. Two strategies for addressing this problem are currently being studied. One has been to dramatically improve the efficiency of irrigation systems by introducing new irrigation technologies.

A farmer tends his fields, which are irrigated by water from the Nile.

New Irrigation Technologies

Hydrologists and agronomists point out that since the 1990s, prospects for improving irrigation by applying new technologies have been promising. The blistering heat of the Lower Nile basin evaporates water from the irrigation trenches so fast that an estimated 40 percent of all water delivered to the fields evaporates before reaching the roots of the plants. Furthermore, because the trenches are simply cut into the ground the water that reaches the plants is unevenly distributed; the plants closest to the inflow are saturated far more than those at the far end of the irrigation trench. To decrease water loss in the fields and to distribute the water more evenly, farmers are replacing long open irrigation ditches with large-scale sprinklers, drip water systems, and plastic coverings for crops.

Sprinkler irrigation systems use less water than ditches and provide better water control. Rather than flooding ditches, long mobile sprinkler systems pump water through pipes to evenly spaced sprinkler heads. These sprinklers spray droplets of water down on the crops as the sprinkler system moves through a field, allowing moisture to reach the root level of the crop. Although these large systems are expensive to build, they pay for themselves by reducing waste of costly water. Although such systems are designed for use on large farms, they are practical when several farmers purchase one system and share it.

Drip water systems are even more efficient at conserving water than sprinklers because they deliver water directly to the root area of each plant by means of narrow plastic tubes. This method ensures a minimum loss of water through evaporation or percolation into the ground. Drip systems are especially efficient for watering tree or vine crops such as dates, figs, grapes, and olives, which have deep roots and which do not require the kind of cultivation that would disturb the water lines. Drip systems are cheaper to purchase than large sprinkler systems but require a great deal of labor to install. Once in place, however, the costs drop dramatically. Plastic lines last for many years and the pumps are inexpensive because the systems operate on low water pressure.

A third water-saving technology is the use of plastic sheets placed over newly planted rows, enveloping the seeds and small plants and preventing the evaporation of water. The plastic sheets are on large rolls that are played out either from behind a tractor or by hand immediately following the planting of seeds. As the new plants are watered, either by a drip system or by an irrigation trench, the water that would ordinarily evaporate is captured under the plastic covering and drips back on the plants when nighttime temperatures drop.

A Canal in the Sudd

Although Egyptian officials who deal with water resources know they cannot expect to increase the amount of water entering the Upper Nile, they think they have found a way to make sure more of that water gets to Egypt. This strategy involves decreasing the White Nile's loss of water to evaporation in the Sudd. To accomplish this objective, the governments of Egypt and Sudan agreed to the construction of the Jonglei Canal, which would provide increased irrigation water for both countries.

Half of the water of the White Nile is congested in the thick bogs of the Sudd in southern Sudan, where the sun's rays evaporate it at the daily rate of millions of gallons. In Egypt's search for ever-increasing amounts of water for crop irrigation, government officials viewed the Sudd as a potential source of water. Egyptian engineers theorized that if a canal could be built siphoning off the water as it enters the Sudd, it could then bypass the swamp and be channeled to northern Sudan and Egypt before it can be lost to evaporation.

In 1978 Sudan and Egypt struck a deal on the construction of the Jonglei Canal, agreeing to share the water equally, which was an anticipated 5 billion cubic yards of water annually, roughly one-quarter of the Sudd water. The large canal would be 210 feet wide and have an average depth of 16 feet and a projected length of 225 miles. The benefits of the Jonglei would have been felt over a wide area in both countries, and the project was to have

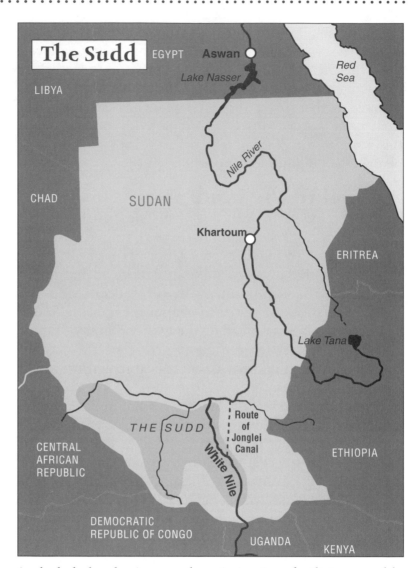

The Sudd

EGYPT Aswan
Lake Nasser
Red Sea
LIBYA
CHAD
SUDAN
Nile River
Khartoum
ERITREA
Lake Tana
THE SUDD
Route of Jonglei Canal
CENTRAL AFRICAN REPUBLIC
White Nile
ETHIOPIA
DEMOCRATIC REPUBLIC OF CONGO
UGANDA
KENYA

included developing modern irrigation facilities capable of converting hundreds of square miles of desert into farmland. The canal planners also estimated that by reducing the amount of water going into the Sudd, they could shrink the swamp and create excellent pastureland for cattle. The canal itself, meanwhile, would provide new opportunities for people to catch fish.

Construction began in 1980, and by 1983 the canal stretched for 160 of the intended 225 miles. Work on the canal had to be halted, however, when militant members of tribes inhabiting the Sudd used a rocket to blow up the huge five-story-tall rotary digger that was carving out the canal. Tribespeople in the region had never been consulted on the building of the canal. As a

The Tragedy of the Jonglei Canal

The termination of work on the Jonglei Canal in 1983 came as a blow to the residents of the Sudd, to Sudan as a whole, and to Egypt. According to the project's research team, the benefits would have been felt over a wide area. The project was to have developed modern irrigation and drainage facilities that would have put an end to agriculture being tied to the annual patterns of flooding and drought. The termination of the project also led to a considerable loss of livestock. According to the estimates of a national conference on peace in 1989, nearly 6.6 million head of cattle perished.

The Jonglei Canal region is inhabited by around 2 million people, mainly the peoples and tribes of the Dinka, Nuer, and Shalak. The local economy is very much a seasonal one. In the rainy season, starting in April or May and lasting until December, rivers flood and people move to higher ground, where they cultivate crops dependent on rain. In January people move once more to the plains, staying for the duration of the dry period. The yearly flooding exposes livestock, as well as humans, to disease and even death, as happened on a large scale during the 1960s. One of the most significant benefits of the project was that it would have curbed the annual flooding and changed the primary features of the region's economy by introducing mechanical agriculture and other means of modernization.

By diverting water away from the Sudd, a part of the land that has been under water for more than twenty years would have been reclaimed, providing ideal ground for breeding cattle. The technical know-how that was to have come to the region would have benefited the Sudd, allowing the government to realize its plans for social and economic development in an area that is unable to fund such development by itself. The project would also have helped with the establishment of an irrigation project to produce crops over an area of about two hundred thousand acres.

result, the environmental studies indicating they would have more grazing land for their cattle had little credibility. Many farming on the edges of the Sudd feared the canal might instead cause widespread poverty.

Although destruction of the digging equipment was sufficient to halt the project temporarily, officials in both Egypt and Sudan remain confident that the canal will eventually be completed.

Fair Treatment for Displaced Native Peoples

The incident highlighted the importance of involving all concerned parties and fairly compensating those who are to be displaced when the Nile's flow is to be altered. Whenever dams or canals are built, the changes in the Nile's flow mean that people living nearby will be impacted in some way. In some cases, such as the tribes of the Sudd, people are becoming increasingly militant when faced with the potential loss of homes, farmland, and pastureland.

Alterations to the natural flow of the Nile have had a socially destructive effect on large numbers of people. Following the building of the Aswan High Dam, for example, thousands of displaced persons rioted over what they perceived to be unfair treatment by both the Egyptian and Sudanese governments.

The experiences of Egyptian and Sudanese officials is being taken as a lesson by governments elsewhere in Africa that are considering the construction of new dams and canals. Kader Asmal, South Africa's minister of education and the former minister of water affairs and forestry, raised this issue in a 1999 conference on dams by saying,

> Another issue is how to encompass not just those directly affected—like those being resettled—but also the larger groups affected downstream. After all, the most directly affected are the poorest of the poor, who are very rarely organized and have very few people to speak on their behalf.[18]

Governments are now requiring public discussions of new water projects with all people who might be displaced. They are also now offering more incentives for people to move, including purchasing their land for a fair price, paying all costs of moving to new lands, and providing educational training for displaced farmers who wish to seek jobs in cities. A good example of this change in policy involves officials of Uganda and the construction of the Bujagali Dam. For five years prior to the start of construction, the Ugandan minister of water and executives of the company constructing the dam held meetings in dozens of cities and towns to discuss the impact of the dam. The focus of most meetings was concerns about how many people would be displaced by the dam, how much money they would receive for their land, and training for those who chose to leave farming to find work in cities.

Alternatives to the Nile

In view of all the problems people along the river are facing, an increasing number of scientists and environmentalists assert that the countries along the Nile have become too dependent on the river. These advocates for the Nile argue that the river has been overexploited and that it is time for all Nile nations to look beyond the Nile to fill their electrical and water needs.

Given that further dam construction on the Nile is a diminishing option, planners in Egypt and elsewhere are looking for new ways to increase the supply of electricity. The most expeditious way to increase the availability of electricity is to prevent its loss. Egyptian electrical engineers estimate, for example, that 30 to 40 percent of the power distributed through the nation's aging electrical grid is lost before it can reach the consumer. They believe much of the loss can be avoided, and they are presently spending money to install new, better-insulated wire, and to shorten the distance electricity needs to travel over the wires. Engineers are also

A researcher in Egypt experiments with solar arrays as an alternative to hydroelectric dams.

developing computerized control systems that efficiently control the electrical load that courses through electrical lines.

But engineers also are working on new sources of electricity. They observe that since many of the Nile nations bask in the sun most of the year, solar generation is becoming a viable alternative to hydroelectric power. Large fields of solar cells are being installed for the first time in the desert wastelands to capture the rays of the sun and convert them into electricity. Although solar electricity costs more to generate, engineers believe these costs will decline over time as more efficient systems are developed.

The Nile Basin Initiative

Even though individual changes in the way water is used and electricity is generated can help solve some of the river's problems, healing the Nile will also require considerable cooperation among all ten nations that share its water. In 1992 the ten Nile nations assembled their ministers of water for the first time to promote cooperation and economic development in the basin. After several years of increasing conflict over water and population displacement, all nations finally recognized the need for an oversight committee to review and inspect all proposed projects on the Nile. The ministers formally established the Nile Basin Initiative (NBI). Its charter is "to achieve sustainable socio-economic development through the equitable utilization of, and benefit from, the common Nile Basin water resources."[19]

As part of the NBI, six of the countries—Egypt, Rwanda, Sudan, Uganda, Tanzania, and the Democratic Republic of the Congo—formed the Technical Cooperation Committee for the Promotion of the Development and Environmental Protection of the Nile Basin. The other four nations—Ethiopia, Eritrea, Burundi, and Kenya—chose to be observers rather than participants.

The Nile Basin Initiative Objectives

The focus on the Nile for the twenty-first century includes not only water resources but also the need for cooperation among the ten member nations of the Nile basin. The website for the Nile Basin Initiative posts the following objectives, which reflect the organization's present concerns:

- To develop the water resources of the Nile basin in a sustainable and equitable way to ensure prosperi-ty, security, and peace for all of its peoples.

- To ensure efficient water management and the optimal use of the resources.

- To ensure cooperation and joint action between the riparian countries, seeking win-win gains.

- To target poverty eradication and promote economic integration.

- To ensure that the program results in a move from planning to action.

To achieve the objectives of the NBI, representatives of the ten Nile nations convene whenever they determine a need to review the benefits and liabilities posed by proposed projects on the Nile. In this way, all member nations, including those living downriver from a proposed project, will know what impact a change may have for the entire length of the river. Thus far, the NBI has experienced considerable success in resolving potential conflicts over the construction of new dams and some limited success in regulating the dumping of toxic materials into the river.

The NBI is currently focused on three major objectives. The first is to enhance everyone's awareness of the socioeconomic, technical, environmental, legal, and organizational aspects of actions affecting the water resources in the Nile basin. The second is to remedy the water and wildlife problems in Lake Victoria caused by industrial and human activities. According to Nancy Chege of the Worldwatch Institute, who studied Lake Victoria and the Upper Nile, "There is a consensus among scientists that if an accelerated push to save the lake is not made soon, this much-needed body of water will cease to sustain life."[20] The third objective is to monitor the construction of the Bujagali Dam in Uganda to ensure that it meets all agreed-upon environmental standards and that all displaced peoples are properly compensated.

Most of the ten member nations to the NBI are optimistic that this is an excellent forum for resolving conflicts over the use of the Nile as well as for maintaining the river as a life-giving natural resource. Nonetheless, they also realize that recent attempts to save the river have come late and many of the suggestions for improvement are on a small scale. At this time, the greatest hope for healing the Nile is the recognition on the part of 300 million people who depend on its continued flow that solutions must be found even if those solutions require some personal sacrifice.

The Nile in the Twenty-First Century

Despite the best intentions of the nations along the Nile, at the dawn of the twenty-first century the demographic reality is that the population growth in the Nile basin is predicted to double to 600 million by the year 2025. All hydrologists, agronomists, and environmentalists recognize that the Nile cannot sustain such growth.

The problems of the Nile and the nations through which it flows are compounded by the fact that of the ten countries that share the Nile, four are among the ten poorest in the world and the others are also struggling financially. Given such dire economic circumstances, generating the money needed to apply expensive new technologies that will begin to clean up the Nile's water, such as water filtration plants, and building new facilities that will continue to meet the increasing demand for water, such as the Jonglei Canal, are daunting challenges.

Yet even if limited funds could be found to begin to put the Nile on the road to recovery, many believe that until the population growth is slowed, no long-term solutions

Many scientists believe that only by limiting population growth along the Nile can this great natural resource be preserved.

are likely. As an example, Egypt, the wealthiest of the ten, already uses all of the Nile water it is allocated by international treaty, mostly for irrigating crops. The water demand for growing wheat is staggering; it takes 1,000 tons of water, 16 million gallons, to grow a single ton of wheat. As the population along the Nile basin continues to multiply, there is not enough water to grow the food for its expanding population. Researchers for the Inventory of Conflict and Environment, a consortium of scientists and economists who monitor conflicts over natural resources, report about the Nile,

> Present and potential conflict over water in the basin stems from the increased food and agricultural needs generated by a rapidly growing population in the riparian states. All three of the major players, Egypt, Sudan and Ethiopia, publicly stated as recently as February 1997 that their share of the water is insufficient and are demanding the right to use the water as they see fit.[21]

The misuse of the Nile is a classic example of people trying to force a great natural resource to meet their needs instead of living within the limitations of that resource. It is the opinion of the majority of scientists studying the Nile that population growth must be slowed if the Nile is to continue to support life along its four-thousand-mile lifeline.

Whether the twenty-first century will be able to heal the wounds inflicted during the twentieth century is uncertain. There is more pessimism among Nile researchers than optimism because the problems are growing at a time when they should be diminishing. What was initially perceived as a problem of too many dams has now grown to problems of overpopulation, excessive pollution, and conflict over rights to the Nile's water. As the twenty-first century begins, those who rely on this river must take action—and quickly—to save the troubled Nile.

Notes

•••••••

Chapter 1: A River in the Sand

1. Daniel Hillel, *Rivers of Eden.* Oxford, UK: Oxford University Press, 1994, p. 87.

Chapter 2: The Ancient Nile

2. Quoted in David P. Silverman, *Ancient Egypt.* New York: Oxford University Press, 1997, p. 60.
3. Herodotus, *The Persian Wars,* trans. George Rawlinson. New York: Modern Library Series, 1942, pp. 122–23.
4. Quoted in Lionel Casson, *Ancient Egypt.* New York: Time-Life Books, 1965, p. 32.
5. Quoted in Egypt: The Complete Guide, "Hymn to Osiris," www.touregypt.net.

Chapter 3: Harnessing the Nile

6. Herodotus, *The Persian Wars,* p. 118.
7. Herodotus, *The Persian Wars,* pp. 128–29.
8. Hillel, *Rivers of Eden,* p. 122.
9. Quoted in Hillel, *Rivers of Eden,* p. 123.

Chapter 4: The Suffering Nile

10. LDEO Climate Modeling Group, "Long-Term Negative Impacts of Aswan High Dam." http://rainbow.ldeo.columbia.edu.
11. Hillel, *Rivers of Eden,* p. 123.
12. Sayed El-Sayed and Gert L. van Dijken, "The Southeastem Mediterranean Ecosystem Revisited: Thirty Years After the Construction of the Aswan High Dam." www-ocean.tamu.edu.
13. El-Sayed and van Dijken, "The Southeastern Mediterranean Ecosystem Revisited."
14. Quoted in Mahmoud Bakr, "Cleansing the Nile," *Al-Ahram Weekly,* July 16–22, 1998, p. 28

15. Quoted in Yomna Kamel, "Residents Suffer from Nile Pollution," *Middle East Times,* September 10, 1999, p. 53.
16. Quoted in Nancy Chege, "Lake Victoria: A Sick Giant," One World. www.oneworld.net.

Chapter 5: Hope and the Nile

17. Quoted in Fatemah Farag, "Managing Water," December 16, 1999. www.dams.org.
18. Quoted in Farag, "Managing Water."
19. Nile Basin Initiative Mission Statement, Nile Basin Initiative. www.nilebasin.org.
20. Chege, "Lake Victoria."
21. Inventory of Conflict and Environment, "ICE Case Studies: Nile River Dispute." http://gurukul.ucc.american.edu.

For Further Reading

Books

Hussein Fahim, *Dams, People, and Development: The Aswan High Dam Case*. New York: Pergamon, 1981. This book provides a detailed discussion of the building of the Aswan High Dam, its impact on the peoples displaced, the environmental consequences, and the politics involved in getting it built.

Michael Heim, *Aswan*. Trans. J. Maxwell Brownjohn. New York: Alfred A. Knopf, 1973. This work provides a fictional scenario in which the Aswan Dam could fail and the costs in terms of destruction and lives. To write this work, Heim consulted with dam engineers, hydrologists, and seismologists for his research into the weaknesses of the dam. Although it is a fictional account, many politicians and engineers believe that it is a book that should be taken seriously.

Patrick McCully, *Silenced Rivers: The Ecology and Politics of Large Dams*. London: Zed Books, 2001. *Silenced Rivers* explains the history and politics of dam building worldwide and shows why large dams have become the most controversial of technologies. The author explains the ecological impacts of large dams and the human consequences.

Alan Moorehead, *The White Nile*. New York: HarperTrade, July 2000. Although this book was originally published forty years ago, it remains one of the finest books on the White Nile. The book focuses on the period of 1856 through 1899, during which time Europeans discovered and monopolized the Nile region.

Virginia Morell, *Blue Nile: Ethiopia's River of Magic and Mystery*. New York: National Geographic Society, 2001. This book offers an account of the author's experiences on a National Geographic expedition on the Blue Nile River through Ethiopia to the Sudan border. Morell reports action-packed adventure with the stories of various Nile expeditions throughout history. In addition to an excellent account of the history of the river and its peoples, the book contains superb photographs of the river and countryside.

David P. Silverman, *Ancient Egypt*. New York: Oxford University Press, 1997. This book provides an excellent overview of Egyptian history. It is organized into eighteen chapters, which are organized by well-chosen themes in Egyptian history. Accompanying the text are photos of Egyptian art, maps, and historical architecture.

Periodicals

Robert Caputo, "Journey up the Nile," *National Geographic*, May 1985.

Rick Gore, "Pharaohs of the Sun," *National Geographic*, April 2001.

Jean-Daniel Stanley, Franck Goddio, and Gerard Schnepp, "Nile Flooding Sank Two Ancient Cities," *Nature*, July 19, 2001.

Peter Theroux, "The Imperiled Nile Delta," *National Geographic*, January 1997.

Works Consulted

Books

Lionel Casson, *Ancient Egypt*. New York: Time-Life Books, 1965. This book is a comprehensive work on Egypt by one of America's foremost scholars in ancient history. The book contains a thorough history of Egypt as well as the Nile and its importance to the country. The text is well supported by primary sources as well as photos and copies of Egyptian art.

Morris R. Cohen and I.E. Drabkin, *A Source Book in Greek Science*. Cambridge, MA: Harvard University Press, 1958. This work is a compendium of ancient engineering innovations that enabled the Greeks to construct temples, roads, sewers, bridges, and other types of civil engineering projects.

Haggai Erlich and Israel Gershoni, *The Nile*. London: Lynne Rienner, 2000. This book is an anthology of scholarly papers on the politics and cultures of the many countries that rely on the Nile. Each essay addresses a topic relating to the effect the river has had and continues to have on all countries through which it flows.

Gianni Guadalupi, *The Discovery of the Nile*. New York: Stewart, Tabori & Chang, 1997. This large book takes the reader through the history of the Nile from the pharaohs through the many nineteenth-century explorers who sought to both discover the source of the Nile and to enslave the people living along the river. This work provides superb large photos of ancient maps as well as art associated with Egypt and the Nile.

Herodotus, *The Persian Wars*. Trans. George Rawlinson. New York: Modern Library Series, 1942. The first half of this famous work describes Herodotus's travels, and the second half focuses on the Persian invasion of Greece during the early fourth century B.C.

Daniel Hillel, *Rivers of Eden*. Oxford, UK: Oxford University Press, 1994. This work provides an excellent socioeconomic history of the rivers of the Middle East. The Nile is prominently featured in the book.

Paul Howell, Michael Lock, and Stephen Cobb, *The Jonglei Canal: Impact and Opportunity.* Cambridge, UK: Cambridge University Press, 1988. The objective of this book is to present a balanced scientific presentation of all relevant aspects of this very complex canal. The book discusses the canal in detail and presents the many problems that have arisen as a result of its proposal, start, and violent end.

John Waterbury, *Hydropolitics of the Nile Valley.* Syracuse, NY: Syracuse University Press, 1979. This book focuses on the recent politics of the ten Nile nations that are struggling to find amiable solutions to the use of the Nile's water and construction projects that seek to alter the course of the water.

Periodicals

Mahmoud Bakr, "Cleansing the Nile," *Al-Ahram Weekly,* July 16–22, 1998.

John Daniszewski, "Egypt Plans a New Valley to Rival the Nile," *Los Angeles Times,* November 18, 1996.

Yomna Kamel, "Residents Suffer from Nile Pollution," *Middle East Times,* September 10, 1999.

Fred Pearce, "High and Dry in Aswan," *New Scientist,* May 7, 1994.

Laura Jean Penvenne, "Disappearing Delta," *American Scientist,* September/October, 1996.

Websites

Africa News Service (www.vitrade.com). This website provides a variety of political, social, and oxymoronic news stories for the African continent.

Department of Oceanography, Texas A&M University (www-ocean. tamu.edu). This website provides information on the faculty of the Department of Oceanography at Texas A&M and on the research projects in which they are currently engaged. Information on academic programs offered by the department is also available.

Egypt: The Complete Guide (www.touregypt.net). This website is designed primarily for travelers to Egypt, but it also contains many links to articles about Egyptian culture.

International Commission on Large Dams (ICOLD) (http://genepi.louis-jean.com). ICOLD provides information about advances in the planning, design, construction, operation, and maintenance of large dams and their associated civil works by collecting and disseminating relevant information and by studying related technical questions.

Inventory of Conflict and Environment (http://gurukul.ucc.american.edu). This website contains hundreds of case studies and expert testimony about natural resources that are causing conflict around the world. Many of their case studies report on conflict for water along the Nile basin.

LDEO Climate Modeling Group (http://rainbow.ldeo.columbia.edu). This website provides information on the research on the earth's climate being conducted by scientists associated with the Lamont-Doherty Earth Observatory at Columbia University.

Nile Basin Initiative (www.nilebasin.org). The Nile Basin Initiative website provides many excellent links that describe the current status of the Nile basin, new projects, member information, photographs, and activities focused on the preservation of the Nile.

Nile Research Institute (www.nwrc.gov.eg). The Nile Research Institute website provides information to promote the protection and development of the Nile River in a sustainable scientific manner. The website presents information on controlling the quality of the Nile's water and of Lake Nasser, protecting the riverbanks from erosion, developing safe navigation, and utilizing the silt deposits in the Aswan High Dam.

OneWorld International Foundation (www.oneworld.net). This website provides a comprehensive view of this organization, which is dedicated to promoting human rights and equitable sharing of the world's resources. The organization's website offers links to a database of documents on many different topics related to global resources.

People and the Planet (www.peopleandplanet.net). This website provides a global review and gateway into the issues of population, poverty, health, consumption, and the environment for threatened biospheres around the world.

World Commission on Dams (www.dams.org). This website provides comprehensive information on the development of large-scale dams around the world. The views and interests of a wide constituency, including engineers, dam owners, and indigenous peoples affected by the dams are represented in reports accessed through the website.

Index

Picture Credits

About the Author

• •

James Barter received his undergraduate degree in history and classics at the University of California at Berkeley, followed by graduate studies in ancient history and archaeology at the University of Pennsylvania. Mr. Barter has taught history as well as Latin and Greek.

A Fulbright scholar at the American Academy in Rome, Mr. Barter worked on archaeological sites in and around the city as well as on sites in the Naples area. Mr. Barter also has worked and traveled extensively in Greece.

Mr. Barter currently lives in Rancho Santa Fe, California, with his sixteen-year-old daughter, Kalista, who is a student at Torrey Pines High School and works as a soccer referee. Mr. Barter's older daughter, Tiffany, also lives in Rancho Santa Fe, where she teaches violin and has a business arranging live music performances.